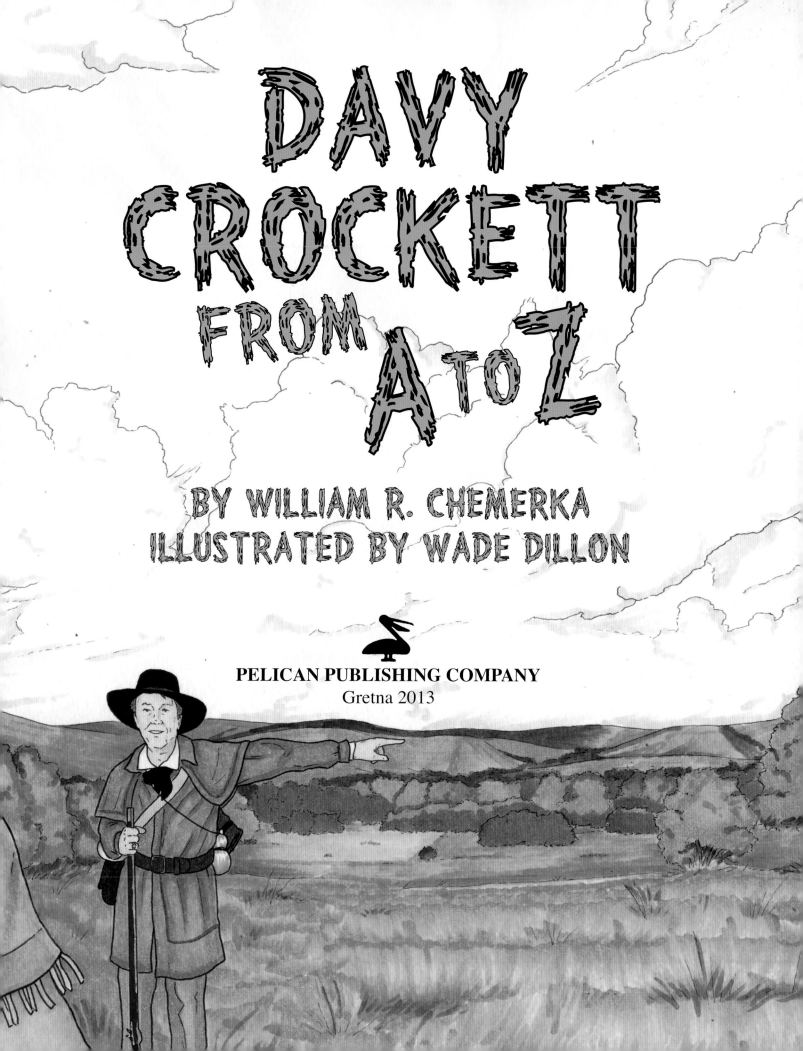

# DAVY CROCKETT FROM A TO Z

## BY WILLIAM R. CHEMERKA
## ILLUSTRATED BY WADE DILLON

PELICAN PUBLISHING COMPANY

Gretna 2013

*To the descendants of David Crocket — W.R.C.*
*To my little lady, Lindsey Otto — W.D.*

---

*The word "Pelican" and the depiction of a pelican are trademarks of Pelican Publishing Company, Inc., and are registered in the U.S. Patent and Trademark Office.*

---

**Library of Congress Cataloging-in-Publication Data**

Chemerka, William R.
  Davy Crockett from A to Z / by William R. Chemerka ; illustrated by Wade Dillon.
    pages cm
  ISBN 978-1-4556-1835-4 (hardcover : alk. paper) — ISBN 978-1-4556-1836-1 (e-book)  1. Crockett, Davy, 1786-1836—Juvenile literature. 2. Pioneers—Tennessee—Biography—Juvenile literature. 3. Legislators—United States—Biography—Juvenile literature. 4. United States. Congress. House—Biography—Juvenile literature. 5. Alamo (San Antonio, Tex.)—Siege, 1836—Juvenile literature. 6. Alphabet books.  I. Dillon, Wade, 1988- illustrator. II. Title.
  F436.C95C48 2013
  976.8'04092--dc23
  [B]

                        2013005712

Printed in Malaysia
Published by Pelican Publishing Company, Inc.
1000 Burmaster Street, Gretna, Louisiana 70053

# A is for Alamo

During the Texas Revolution of 1835-36, Davy Crockett joined
the Texans and Tejanos rebelling against the dictatorship of
Mexican general Santa Anna. The Alamo was an old Spanish
mission in San Antonio, Texas, that had been converted into
a fort. Santa Anna's troops attacked the Alamo on March 6,
1836, and killed all of the defenders, including Crockett.

# B is for Betsy

"Betsy" was the nickname of Crockett's favorite rifle. He used the flintlock weapon primarily for hunting. Crockett also used the rifle at shooting matches where he displayed his expert marksmanship.

# **C** is for Creek Indian War

The Creek Indian War was fought in 1813 and 1814. Crockett volunteered to fight against the Creeks. During the war, Crockett scouted, hunted, and fought in several battles. When the war was over, he returned home to his family.

# D is for David Crockett

The *David Crockett* was an impressive clipper ship that was launched in 1853. It celebrated Crockett's popularity in books, plays, and songs. The ship carried passengers and cargo between New York and San Francisco, and between New York and Liverpool, England.

# **E** is for Esparza

Enrique Esparza was a young boy who resided with his parents and brothers and sister in the Alamo during the famous siege and battle. Esparza remembered that Crockett was "everywhere during the siege and personally slew many of the enemy with his rifle, his pistol and knife."

# F is for Freemasonry

Freemasonry is a fraternal organization that attempts to help good men become better. While he served in Congress, Crockett joined the Masons. Masons, who believe in a Supreme Being, belong to lodges where they host regular meetings. The Davy Crockett Lodge in San Antonio, Texas, is named after the famous frontiersman.

# G is for "Gentleman from the Cane"

"Gentleman from the Cane" was a nickname for Crockett that his political opponents created. They described him as a man who came from the canebrake or backwoods, an area populated by poor people. But Crockett liked the nickname because he was proud of where he lived and the men and women he represented.

# H is for Hat

Crockett is best known for wearing a coonskin hat, which featured the tail of a raccoon. Although he also wore other kinds of hats during his lifetime, Crockett was seen wearing a coonskin hat when he left Tennessee to go to Texas in 1835.

# **I** is for Indian Removal Act

Congressman Davy Crockett opposed the Indian Removal Act, which was signed into law by Pres. Andrew Jackson in 1830. The law forced thousands of Native Americans to leave their homes in the eastern United States and settle on reservations west of the Mississippi River.

# J is for Jackson

Andrew Jackson was Crockett's commander during the Creek War. Jackson was elected president of the United States in 1828 and re-elected in 1832. At first, Crockett supported Jackson, but when the president signed the Indian Removal Act into law, Crockett opposed him and they became political enemies.

# K is for Kitchen

Benjamin Kitchen was the master of a frontier school to which Crockett's father sent him as a boy. But Crockett only spent four days in Kitchen's school. Following a fight with a school mate, Crockett ran away from Kitchen's school and did not return home for several years.

# L is for *Lion of the West*

The *Lion of the West* was a popular play about a frontier character based on Crockett. The play featured Nimrod Wildfire, who wore animal skins and had a razor sharp wit. Crockett saw James Hackett, an actor, perform the role in 1833. When Hackett saw Crockett in the audience,

# M is for Motto

Crockett's motto was: "Be always sure you're right, then go ahead." The phrase appeared in his popular 1834 autobiography. Crockett believed that everyone should carefully think about what they were going to do before they decided to "go ahead."

*I leave This rule for others when I am dead
Be always Sure you are right Then go ahead*

*David Crockett*

# N is for Native Americans

Crockett fought against Native American warriors during the Creek Indian War. However, once the war was over, Crockett defended their rights while he served in Congress. He once nominated a Cherokee to serve as a government agent to the Seminoles residing in Florida.

# O is for Obion River

Crockett established a new home for himself and his family near the Obion River in western Tennessee in 1821. The area around the Obion River, which flows into the Mississippi River, was a rich hunting area. Called the Shakes, the land still showed evidence of a famous 1811 earthquake when Crockett moved there.

# P is for Polly

Mary "Polly" Finley was eighteen years old when she married Davy Crockett in 1806. They had three children: John, William, and Margaret. However, Polly died of illness in 1815.

# Q is for Quaker

When he was fifteen years old, Crockett worked for six months for a Quaker named John Kennedy, whose son taught Crockett the basics of reading, writing, and arithmetic. The Quakers, a group officially known as the Religious Society of Friends, are peaceful people who dress plainly and work hard.

# R is for Red Sticks

The Red Sticks were part of the Creek Nation who waged war on the frontier in 1813 and 1814. Crockett fought against the Red Sticks during the Creek Indian War. When the war ended, the Red Sticks and the other Creeks were forced to give up half their land to the United States.

# S is for Squatters

"Squatters" was the name given to poor people who built homes and farms on unoccupied and unclaimed federal land. Congressman Davy Crockett defended these poor farmers, but Pres. Andrew Jackson wanted the squatters to either pay for the land or leave it.

# T is for Tennessee

Crockett was born in Tennessee on August 17, 1786, at a place near the fork of the Nollichucky River and Limestone Creek. The area in eastern Tennessee where Crockett was born briefly had been called the State of Franklin and was originally part of North Carolina.

# U is for U.S. House of Representatives

Crockett was elected to the U.S. House of Representatives
in 1827 to speak for Tennessee. He was re-elected in 1829,
but lost two years later. Crockett won his final Congressional
election in 1833 but lost again in 1835. It was then that he

# V is for Volunteer

Crockett became a volunteer soldier during the Creek Indian War. After his third and final term in Congress, Crockett traveled to Texas where he volunteered as a private in the army of the Republic of Texas. Crockett's home state of Tennessee is known as the Volunteer State.

# W is for Whig Party

The Whig Party was a political party that formed in 1834. Just like Crockett, the Whigs opposed Pres. Andrew Jackson, who was the leader of the Democratic Party. They claimed that Jackson was acting like a king. In England, the Whig Party is the traditional party of opposition to the king. Crockett supported the Whig Party after Jackson signed the Indian Removal Bill into law.

# X is for Ximenez

Damacio Ximenez was a Tejano, a native-born Texan of Mexican decent, who fought alongside Crockett at the Alamo. He and other Tejano volunteers remained at the Alamo for thirteen days and later fought to the death in the memorable 1836 battle.

# Y is for Yarns

Crockett was well known for telling exciting yarns—stories that were filled with action and adventure. The *Davy Crockett Almanacs*, which were published from 1835 to 1856, added to the Crockett legend by featuring wild and exciting yarns in which he was described riding a streak of lightning and climbing Niagara Falls on the back of an alligator.

# Z is for Zeb

Zeb was a fictional friend of Crockett who appeared in one of the *Crockett Almanacs*. Zeb was described as a "ring-tailed roarer" who enjoyed hunting with his dog. Wild characters like Zeb made the almanacs very popular and helped spread the legend of Davy Crockett throughout the country.

# 100
## cupcakes
## & cakes
### from 1 easy recipe

This edition published in 2011

LOVE FOOD is an imprint of Parragon Books Ltd

Parragon
Queen Street House
4 Queen Street
Bath BA1 1HE, UK

Copyright © Parragon Books Ltd 2009

LOVE FOOD and the accompanying heart device is a registered trade
mark of Parragon Books Ltd in Australia, the UK, USA, India, and the EU.

www.parragon.com

ISBN: 978-1-4454-6257-8

Printed in China

Cover design by Talking Design
Written by Christine France
Internal design by Simon Levy
Photography by Clive Streeter
Home economy by Angela Drake

Notes for the Reader
This book uses standard kitchen measuring spoons and cups. All spoon
and cup measurements are level unless otherwise indicated. Unless
otherwise stated, milk is assumed to be whole, eggs are large, individual
vegetables are medium, and pepper is freshly ground black pepper.

The times given are only an approximate guide. Preparation times differ
according to the techniques used by different people and the cooking
times may also vary from those given. Optional ingredients, variations,
or serving suggestions have not been included in the calculations.

Recipes using raw or very lightly cooked eggs should be avoided by
infants, the elderly, pregnant women, convalescents, and anyone with a
chronic illness. Pregnant and breast-feeding women are advised to avoid
eating peanuts and peanut products. People with nut allergies should be
aware that some of the prepared ingredients used in the recipes in this
book may contain nuts. Always check the packaging before use.

# Contents

# Introduction

Even if you're not a domestic god or goddess, the good news is that home-baked cakes don't have to be difficult or time-consuming. This book is packed with quick-mix cakes for all occasions, so you'll never be short of ideas for easy, irresistible home-baked treats. The beauty of this book is that every single recipe is based on the Basic Cake Mix (see page 10). To make life easier for you, we have done the hard work so that each recipe is complete and you won't need to refer back to the basic recipe every time.

## Equipment

The equipment needed for these cakes is found in most kitchens: mixing bowl, sifter, measuring cups and spoons, a wire cooling rack, and cake pans.

Good-quality cake pans conduct heat evenly and efficiently for perfect results and will last for years. Basic cake pan shapes include deep round and square, layer, tube, Bundt, loaf, springform, muffin, and rectangular. The success of a cake depends on choosing the correct size of pan. Because cake pan sizes vary between manufacturers, the recipes in this book provide the pan's capacity. To find a pan's capacity, simply use a measuring cup to pour water into the pan and note how many cups it takes to fill the pan.

Mixing bowls in tempered glass, melamine, or polyethylene are tough and versatile for mixing. Choose measuring cups and spoons marked clearly in standard measures.

A handheld electric mixer does much of the hard work but you can mix by hand with a wooden spoon if you prefer.

## Basic Ingredients

The basic cake mix includes all-purpose flour, baking powder, butter/oil/cream/yogurt, sugar/honey/syrup, eggs, vanilla or other flavoring extract, and milk or fruit juice.

All-purpose flour is used with baking powder, and these must be sifted together to make sure of even distribution of the rising agent throughout the mixture. Ratios do vary slightly, so always check the quantities in the ingredients list before you start.

Butter gives the best flavor, but it can be replaced by margarine if you prefer. Spreads are usually lower in fat and may produce unreliable results. Use softened butter, either at room temperature and beaten until soft, or softened in a microwave for a few seconds but not melted. Oil is useful when a moist texture is required, such as for gingerbreads, and a light-flavored oil, such as sunflower, is a good choice. Cream and yogurt are lower in fat than butter, so these produce cakes with a denser texture and a shorter life.

Superfine sugar gives a light, fine-textured cake, but natural light or dark brown sugar can be substituted to add an extra richness of flavor. Always make sure that there are no hard lumps in the sugar before adding to the mix because these may not dissolve. Light corn syrup or honey can be used as a substitute for sugar in cakes where a softer texture is required. Raw brown sugar is good for sprinkling over the top to add a crunchy topping. Confectioners' sugar is invaluable for fillings and frostings, or for dusting over cakes as instant decoration.

Eggs should be large, ideally at room temperature. If you store eggs in the refrigerator, remove them about 30 minutes before use to let them come up to room temperature.

Vanilla extract is the most versatile flavoring to enhance cakes and baked goods. For true flavor, make sure to choose bottles marked "extract" rather than "flavoring." Other useful extracts used in this book are almond, coffee, orange flower water, rose water, and peppermint.

Milk or fruit juice is added to lighten the mix, and you can choose whole, low-fat, or skim milk, or fruit juices, such as apple, orange, or lemon. Some recipes may omit this, depending on the balance of added ingredients.

## Extra Ingredients

Whole-wheat flour, oats, or cornmeal may be substituted for some or all of the all-purpose flour or added to the mix to vary the texture and flavor, the amount depending on the balance of other ingredients. Generally, the higher the fiber and coarser the grain, the denser the resulting texture will be.

The simplest way to vary the flavor of cakes is to add spices—cinnamon, apple or pumpkin pie spice, allspice, nutmeg, ginger, and star anise all work well in cakes. Sift the spices with the flour and baking powder to make sure that they're evenly combined with the mix. Finely grated citrus rind will add a light, fresh flavor to many cakes and frostings.

Chocolate cakes are always a favorite and this may be added in the form of unsweetened cocoa powder, chocolate chips, or melted chocolate. It may be necessary to reduce the quantity of flour when adding unsweetened cocoa powder to some cakes, so make sure to check the recipe.

Fresh or dried fruits transform a simple sponge cake into a rich special-occasion cake or luxurious gâteau. Dried fruits have a concentrated flavor and sweetness and they're great pantry standbys. Canned fruit should be drained well, because the extra liquid may upset the recipe balance.

Nuts (such as almonds, hazelnuts, walnuts, or pecans) or seeds (such as sunflower, pumpkin, poppy, or sesame) not only give a crunchy texture to cakes but also add valuable nutrients and fiber for healthier treats.

## Top Tips for Successful Cakes

- Turn on the oven before you start in order to preheat it to the correct temperature while you're mixing.

- Brush cake pans with melted butter or oil and line with nonstick parchment paper to prevent sticking.

- Measure ingredients accurately and level measuring cups and spoons flat with the back of a knife.

- Avoid overmixing because this can cause a heavy texture—beat the mix until just smooth.

- Bake the cake immediately once mixed, because the baking powder begins to act as soon as it's combined with liquid.

- Avoid opening the oven door too often during baking—this reduces the oven temperature and can cause cakes to sink.

- Test cakes carefully for doneness—they should be well risen and golden brown and starting to shrink from the sides of the pan. Sponge cakes should feel springy to the touch.

- To prevent damage, let cakes stand in the pan to firm up for a few minutes before turning out onto a wire rack to finish cooling.

# Basic Cake Mix

**Makes 2 x 8-inch/20-cm sponge layer cakes**

- ✳ oil or melted butter, for greasing
- ✳ 1¹/₂ cups all-purpose flour
- ✳ 1 tbsp baking powder
- ✳ ³/₄ cup unsalted butter, softened (recipes may substitute oil, cream, or yogurt)
- ✳ generous ³/₄ cup superfine sugar (recipes may substitute brown sugar or honey/syrup)
- ✳ 3 eggs
- ✳ 1 tsp vanilla extract (recipes may substitute other flavoring extracts, e.g. almond, coffee, or orange flower water)
- ✳ 2 tbsp milk or fruit juice

This is the basic recipe that all 100 variations of cakes in the book are based on.

For each recipe the basic mix is highlighted (✳) for easy reference, so all you have to do is follow the easy steps each time and you'll never run out of ideas for creative cakes.

Please note that the basic ingredients may vary from time to time so please check these carefully.

# Favorites

# Chocolate Layer Cake

1. Preheat the oven to 350°F/180°C. Grease and line the bottoms of two 8-inch/20-cm layer cake pans.

2. Sift the flour, cocoa, and baking powder into a large bowl and add the butter, superfine sugar, eggs, and vanilla extract. Beat well until the mixture is smooth, then stir in the milk.

3. Divide the mixture between the prepared pans and smooth the surfaces with a spatula. Bake in the preheated oven for 25–30 minutes, or until golden brown and firm to the touch. Let cool in the pans for 2–3 minutes, then turn out and finish cooling on a wire rack.

4. When the cakes have cooled completely, sandwich them together with the chocolate spread, then dust with confectioners' sugar and serve.

**Serves 8**

* oil or melted butter, for greasing

1⅓ cups all-purpose flour

2 tbsp unsweetened cocoa

* 1 tbsp baking powder

* ¾ cup unsalted butter, softened

* generous ¾ cup superfine sugar

* 3 eggs, beaten

* 1 tsp vanilla extract

* 2 tbsp milk

⅔ cup chocolate spread

confectioners' sugar, for dusting

# Coffee & Walnut Ring

1. Preheat the oven to 325°F/160°C. Grease a 6¾-cup tube cake pan, preferably nonstick.

2. Sift the flour and baking powder into a large bowl and add the butter, sugar, eggs, and coffee extract. Beat well until the mixture is smooth, then stir in the chopped walnuts.

3. Spoon the mixture into the prepared pan and smooth the surface with a spatula. Bake in the preheated oven for 40–45 minutes, or until risen, firm, and golden brown.

4. Let cool in the pan for 10 minutes, then turn out carefully onto a wire rack. While the cake is still warm, spoon over half the maple syrup. To serve, top with walnut halves and drizzle with the remaining maple syrup.

**Serves 10**

* oil or melted butter, for greasing
* 1½ cups all-purpose flour
* 1 tbsp baking powder
* ¾ cup unsalted butter, softened
* generous ¾ cup light brown sugar
* 3 eggs, beaten
* 1 tsp coffee extract
  ⅔ cup chopped walnuts
  4 tbsp maple syrup
  walnut halves, to decorate

# Sticky Ginger Loaf

1 Preheat the oven to 350°F/180°C. Grease and line a 5-cup loaf pan.

2 Sift the flour, baking powder, and ground ginger into a large bowl. Add the oil, sugar, corn syrup, and eggs, then beat well to a smooth batter. Stir in the chopped ginger.

3 Pour the mixture into the prepared pan. Bake in the preheated oven for 1–1¼ hours, or until well risen and firm.

4 Let cool in the pan for 10 minutes, then turn out and finish cooling on a wire rack. To serve, brush the cake with the ginger syrup, arrange the sliced ginger on top, and cut into slices.

**Serves 8–10**

✳ oil or melted butter, for greasing

✳ 1½ cups all-purpose flour

✳ 1 tbsp baking powder

1 tbsp ground ginger

✳ ¾ cup sunflower oil

scant ½ cup dark brown sugar

⅓ cup dark corn syrup

✳ 3 eggs, beaten

3 pieces preserved ginger in syrup, drained and finely chopped, plus 2 tbsp syrup from the jar

sliced preserved ginger, to decorate

# Chocolate Fudge Cake

1. Preheat the oven to 350°F/180°C. Grease and line a 9-inch/23-cm round cake pan.

2. Put the chocolate and milk into a small pan and heat gently until melted, without boiling. Remove from the heat.

3. Sift the flour and baking powder into a large bowl and add the butter, brown sugar, eggs, and vanilla extract. Beat well until smooth, then stir in the melted chocolate mixture, mixing evenly.

4. Spoon the mixture into the prepared pan and smooth the top level. Bake in the preheated oven for 50–60 minutes, or until firm to the touch and just beginning to shrink away from the sides of the pan.

5. Let cool in the pan for 10 minutes, then turn out and finish cooling on a wire rack. When cold, carefully slice the cake horizontally into 2 layers.

6. For the frosting, melt the chocolate with the butter in a small pan over low heat. Remove from the heat and stir in the confectioners' sugar, vanilla extract, and milk, then beat well until smooth.

7. Sandwich the cake layers together with half the frosting, then spread the remainder on top of the cake, swirling with a spatula. Sprinkle with the grated chocolate before serving.

**Serves 8**

* oil or melted butter, for greasing
  2 oz/55 g semisweet chocolate
* 2 tbsp milk
* 1½ cups all-purpose flour
* 1 tbsp baking powder
* ¾ cup unsalted butter, softened
* generous ¾ cup dark brown sugar
* 3 eggs, beaten
* 1 tsp vanilla extract
  grated chocolate, to decorate

**Frosting**
3½ oz/100 g semisweet chocolate
¼ cup unsalted butter, softened
1½ cups confectioners' sugar
1 tsp vanilla extract
1 tbsp milk

# 5

# Marbled Chocolate & Vanilla Ring

1. Preheat the oven to 325°F/160°C. Grease a 6¾-cup tube cake pan, preferably nonstick.

2. Sift the flour and baking powder into a large bowl and add the butter, superfine sugar, and eggs. Beat well until the mixture is smooth. Transfer half the mixture to a separate bowl.

3. Combine the cocoa and milk and stir into one bowl of mixture. Add the vanilla extract to the other bowl and mix evenly. Spoon alternate tablespoons of the 2 mixtures into the prepared pan and swirl lightly with a spatula for a marbled effect.

4. Bake in the preheated oven for 40–50 minutes, or until risen, firm, and golden brown. Let cool in the pan for 10 minutes, then turn out and finish cooling on a wire rack. Dust with confectioners' sugar before serving.

**Serves 12**

* oil or melted butter, for greasing
* 1½ cups all-purpose flour
* 1 tbsp baking powder
* ¾ cup unsalted butter, softened
* generous ¾ cup superfine sugar
* 3 eggs, beaten
  2 tbsp unsweetened cocoa
* 2 tbsp milk
* 1 tsp vanilla extract
  confectioners' sugar, for dusting

# Banana Cake with Caramel Frosting

1. Preheat the oven to 325°F/160°C. Grease and line an 8-inch/20-cm square, deep cake pan.

2. Sift the flour and baking powder into a large bowl and add the butter, sour cream, brown sugar, eggs, and vanilla extract. Beat well until the mixture is smooth. Stir in the bananas.

3. Spoon the mixture into the prepared pan and smooth the surface with a spatula. Bake in the preheated oven for about 1 hour, or until risen and golden brown.

4. Let cool in the pan for 10 minutes, then turn out and finish cooling on a wire rack.

5. For the frosting, put the butter and brown sugar into a pan and simmer gently, stirring, for about 2 minutes. Remove from the heat and beat in the sour cream and confectioners' sugar. Let cool for 30–40 minutes, or until thick enough to hold its shape.

6. Spread the frosting over the top of the cake, swirling with a knife.

**Serves 12**

* oil or melted butter, for greasing
* 1½ cups all-purpose flour
* 1 tbsp baking powder
  ⅓ cup unsalted butter, softened
  ⅓ cup sour cream
* generous ¾ cup light brown sugar
* 3 eggs, beaten
* 1 tsp vanilla extract
  2 ripe bananas, mashed

Frosting
3 tbsp unsalted butter
3 tbsp light brown sugar
2 tbsp sour cream
¾ cup confectioners' sugar

# Sponge Roll

1. Preheat the oven to 350°F/180°C. Grease and line a 9 x 13-inch/23 x 33-cm jelly roll pan with the paper ½ inch/ 1 cm above the rim. Lay a sheet of parchment paper on the counter and sprinkle with superfine sugar.

2. Sift the flour and baking powder into a large bowl and add the butter, sugar, eggs, and vanilla extract. Beat well until the mixture is smooth, then beat in the milk.

3. Spoon the mixture into the prepared pan and smooth into the corners with a spatula. Bake in the preheated oven for 15–20 minutes, or until risen, firm, and golden brown.

4. When baked, carefully turn out the sponge cake onto the sugared parchment paper and spread with the jelly. Roll up the sponge cake firmly from one short side to enclose the jelly, keeping the paper around the outside to hold it in place.

5. Lift onto a wire rack to cool, removing the paper when firm. Sprinkle with superfine sugar, cut into slices, and serve.

**Serves 8**

* oil or melted butter, for greasing
  1⅓ cups all-purpose flour
  1½ tsp baking powder
* ¾ cup unsalted butter, softened
* generous ¾ cup superfine sugar, plus extra for sprinkling
* 3 eggs, beaten
* 1 tsp vanilla extract
* 2 tbsp milk
  scant ½ cup raspberry jelly, warmed

# Date & Spice Loaf

1. Preheat the oven to 325°F/160°C. Grease and line a 5⅔-cup loaf pan.

2. Sift the flours, baking powder, and apple pie spice into a large bowl, adding any bran left in the sifter. Add the butter, sugar, eggs, and vanilla extract. Beat well until the mixture is smooth. Stir in half the dates.

3. Spoon the mixture into the prepared pan and sprinkle with the remaining dates. Bake in the preheated oven for 40–50 minutes, or until risen and golden brown.

4. Let cool in the pan for 10 minutes, then turn out and finish cooling on a wire rack.

**Serves 8–10**

* oil or melted butter, for greasing
* ¾ cup all-purpose flour
* generous ¾ cup whole-wheat flour
* 1 tbsp baking powder
* 1 tsp apple pie spice
* ¾ cup unsalted butter, softened
* generous ¾ cup superfine sugar
* 3 eggs, beaten
* 1 tsp vanilla extract
* 1¼ cups coarsely chopped pitted dried dates

# Fig & Lemon Bars

① Preheat the oven to 325°F/160°C. Grease and line an 8 x 12-inch/20 x 30-cm rectangular cake pan.

② Put the figs, lemon juice, water, and raw brown sugar into a pan and bring to a boil. Reduce the heat, cover, and simmer gently, stirring occasionally, for 5 minutes, or until the liquid is absorbed. Remove from the heat and beat lightly to make a coarse puree.

③ Sift the flour, baking powder, and cinnamon into a large bowl and add the butter, light brown sugar, and eggs. Beat well until the mixture is smooth. Stir in the lemon rind.

④ Spoon the mixture into the prepared pan and smooth the surface with a spatula. Spoon the fig puree over the top and swirl it into the cake mixture with a knife. Bake in the preheated oven for 40–50 minutes, or until risen and golden brown.

⑤ Let cool in the pan for 20 minutes, then turn out and finish cooling on a wire rack. When completely cool, cut into bars and serve.

**Makes 8–10**

✳ oil or melted butter, for greasing

generous 1 cup chopped dried figs

✳ 2 tbsp lemon juice

½ cup water

1 tbsp raw brown sugar

✳ 1½ cups all-purpose flour

2 tsp baking powder

1 tsp ground cinnamon

✳ ¾ cup unsalted butter, softened

✳ generous ¾ cup light brown sugar

✳ 3 eggs, beaten

finely grated rind of 1 lemon

# Country Fruit Cake

1. Preheat the oven to 325°F/160°C. Grease and line an 8-inch/20-cm round, deep cake pan.

2. Sift the flours, baking powder, and nutmeg into a large bowl, adding any bran left in the sifter. Add the butter, light brown sugar, eggs, and vanilla extract. Beat well until the mixture is smooth, then stir in the milk and mixed dried fruit.

3. Spoon the mixture into the prepared pan and smooth level with a spatula. Sprinkle the raw brown sugar evenly over the surface. Bake in the preheated oven for 1 hour 20 minutes– 1 hour 30 minutes, or until risen, firm, and golden brown.

4. Let cool in the pan for about 20 minutes, then turn out and finish cooling on a wire rack.

**Serves 10**

* oil or melted butter, for greasing
* 1½ cups all-purpose flour
  ⅔ cup whole-wheat flour
  2 tsp baking powder
  ½ tsp ground nutmeg
* ¾ cup unsalted butter, softened
* generous ¾ cup light brown sugar
* 3 eggs, beaten
* 1 tsp vanilla extract
  1 tbsp milk
  1⅓ cups mixed dried fruit
  1 tbsp raw brown sugar

# Vanilla Sponge Layer Cake

1. Preheat the oven to 350°F/180°C. Grease and line the bottoms of two 8-inch/20-cm layer cake pans.

2. Sift the flour and baking powder into a large bowl and add the butter, superfine sugar, eggs, and vanilla extract. Beat well until the mixture is smooth, then stir in the milk.

3. Divide the mixture between the prepared pans and smooth the surfaces with a spatula. Bake in the preheated oven for 25–30 minutes, or until risen, firm, and golden brown. Let cool in the pans for 2–3 minutes, then turn out and finish cooling on a wire rack.

4. For the filling, beat together the butter, confectioners' sugar, and vanilla extract until smooth. Spread this mixture on top of one of the cakes and the bottom of the other with the jelly, then sandwich the two cakes together to enclose the filling, pressing down lightly.

5. Dust the cake with confectioners' sugar before serving.

**Serves 6–8**

* oil or melted butter, for greasing
* 1½ cups all-purpose flour
* 1 tbsp baking powder
* ¾ cup unsalted butter, softened
* generous ¾ cup superfine sugar
* 3 eggs, beaten
* 1 tsp vanilla extract
* 2 tbsp milk

**Filling**
¼ cup unsalted butter, softened
1 cup confectioners' sugar, plus extra for dusting
½ tsp vanilla extract
3 tbsp strawberry jelly

# Carrot Cake with Orange Frosting

1. Preheat the oven to 325°F/160°C. Grease and line a 9-inch/23-cm round, deep cake pan.

2. Sift the flour, baking powder, cinnamon, and ginger into a bowl and add the butter, sugar, and eggs. Beat well until smooth, then stir in the orange juice, carrots, and chopped pecans.

3. Spoon the mixture into the prepared pan and spread the top level. Bake in the preheated oven for 1 hour–1 hour 10 minutes, or until well risen, firm, and golden brown.

4. Let cool in the pan for 10 minutes, then turn out onto a wire rack to finish cooling.

5. For the frosting, put all the ingredients into a bowl and beat until smooth and thick, adding more orange juice if necessary. Spread over the top of the cake and decorate with pecan halves.

**Serves 10**

* oil or melted butter, for greasing
* 1½ cups all-purpose flour
* 1 tbsp baking powder
* 1 tsp ground cinnamon
* ½ tsp ground ginger
* ¾ cup unsalted butter, softened
* generous ¾ cup light brown sugar
* 3 eggs, beaten
* 2 tbsp orange juice
* scant 1½ cups coarsely grated carrots
* ½ cup chopped pecans
* pecan halves, to decorate

## Frosting
¼ cup whole-fat cream cheese
2¼ cups confectioners' sugar
finely grated rind of 1 orange
1 tbsp orange juice, plus extra if needed

# 13

# Honey & Poppy Seed Ring

1. Preheat the oven to 325°F/160°C. Grease a 6¾-cup tube cake pan, preferably nonstick.

2. Sift the flour and baking powder into a large bowl and add the butter, sugar, 4 tablespoons of the honey, the eggs, and vanilla extract. Beat well until the mixture is smooth. Stir in the poppy seeds and lemon juice.

3. Spoon the mixture into the prepared pan and smooth the surface with a spatula. Bake in the preheated oven for 40–50 minutes, or until risen and golden brown.

4. Let cool in the pan for 20 minutes, then turn out carefully and finish cooling on a wire rack. To serve, warm the remaining 2 tablespoons of the honey and drizzle it over the cake, then cut into slices and serve.

**Serves 12**

✳ oil or melted butter, for greasing
✳ 1½ cups all-purpose flour
✳ 1 tbsp baking powder
✳ ¾ cup unsalted butter, softened
   ½ cup superfine sugar
   6 tbsp honey
✳ 3 eggs, beaten
✳ 1 tsp vanilla extract
   2 tbsp poppy seeds
✳ 2 tbsp lemon juice

14

# Lemon Drizzle Loaf

1. Preheat the oven to 350°F/180°C. Grease and line a 5-cup loaf pan.

2. Sift the flour and baking powder into a large bowl and add the butter, superfine sugar, eggs, and egg yolk. Beat well until the mixture is smooth, then stir in the lemon rind and juice.

3. Spoon the mixture into the prepared pan and smooth the surface with a spatula. Bake in the preheated oven for 40–50 minutes, or until well risen and golden brown.

4. Remove the pan from the oven and transfer to a wire rack. For the syrup, put the confectioners' sugar and lemon juice into a pan and heat gently without boiling, stirring, until the sugar dissolves.

5. Prick the top of the loaf several times with a skewer and spoon the syrup over it. Let cool completely in the pan, then turn out, sprinkle with strips of lemon zest, and serve in slices.

**Serves 8–10**

* oil or melted butter, for greasing
* 1½ cups all-purpose flour
* 1 tbsp baking powder
* ¾ cup unsalted butter, softened
* generous ¾ cup superfine sugar
* 3 eggs, beaten
* 1 egg yolk
* finely grated rind of 1 lemon
* 2 tbsp lemon juice
* fine strips of lemon zest, to decorate

**Syrup**
¾ cup confectioners' sugar
3 tbsp lemon juice

# Hazelnut Crumble Bars

1. Preheat the oven to 325°F/160°C. Grease and line an 8 x 12-inch/20 x 30-cm rectangular cake pan.

2. Sift the flour and baking powder into a large bowl and add the butter, light brown sugar, eggs, vanilla extract, and chocolate spread. Beat well until the mixture is smooth. Stir in the hazelnuts.

3. Spread the mixture into the prepared pan and smooth the surface with a spatula. For the topping, combine the flour and chocolate spread to make a crumbly texture, then stir in the raw brown sugar and hazelnuts. Spread the topping over the cake mixture.

4. Bake in the preheated oven for 40–50 minutes, or until risen and firm. Let cool in the pan before cutting into bars.

**Makes 12**

- oil or melted butter, for greasing
- 1½ cups all-purpose flour
- 2 tsp baking powder
- ½ cup unsalted butter, softened
- generous ¾ cup light brown sugar
- 3 eggs, beaten
- 1 tsp vanilla extract
- ¼ cup chocolate hazelnut spread
- ½ cup chopped hazelnuts

**Topping**
- scant ½ cup all-purpose flour
- ¼ cup chocolate hazelnut spread
- 2 tbsp raw brown sugar
- ⅓ cup chopped hazelnuts

# 16

# Applesauce Cake

1. Preheat the oven to 350°F/180°C. Grease and line the bottoms of two 8-inch/20-cm layer cake pans.

2. Sift the flour, cornstarch, and baking powder into a large bowl and add the butter, sugar, eggs, and vanilla extract. Beat well until the mixture is smooth. Stir in ⅓ cup of the applesauce.

3. Divide the mixture between the prepared pans and smooth the surfaces with a spatula. Bake in the preheated oven for 25–30 minutes, or until risen, firm, and golden brown.

4. Let cool in the pans for 5 minutes, then turn out carefully and finish cooling on a wire rack. Use the remaining applesauce to sandwich the cakes together.

5. Core and thinly slice the apple and brush with lemon juice. Arrange the slices on top of the cake to decorate, then sprinkle with a little superfine sugar.

**Serves 6**

* oil or melted butter, for greasing
* 1½ cups all-purpose flour
  1 tbsp cornstarch
* 1 tbsp baking powder
* ¾ cup unsalted butter, softened
* generous ¾ cup superfine sugar, plus extra for sprinkling
* 3 eggs, beaten
* 1 tsp vanilla extract
  scant 1 cup applesauce or thick apple puree
  1 apple
  lemon juice, for brushing

# 17

# Prune & Walnut Swirl Cake

1. Preheat the oven to 325°F/160°C. Grease and line a 7½-inch/19-cm square, deep cake pan.

2. Put the prunes into a pan with the apple juice, bring to a boil, then reduce the heat and simmer for 8–10 minutes, until the liquid is absorbed. Process the prune mixture in a food processor or blender to a smooth, thick puree.

3. Sift the flour and baking powder into a large bowl and add the butter, sugar, eggs, and vanilla extract. Beat well until the mixture is smooth. Reserve 2 tablespoons of the walnuts, then stir the remainder into the cake mixture.

4. Spoon the mixture into the prepared pan, then drop spoonfuls of the prune puree over the top. Swirl into the cake mix with a knife and smooth the surface level. Sprinkle the reserved walnuts over the cake.

5. Bake in the preheated oven for 1 hour–1 hour 10 minutes, or until risen, firm, and golden brown. Let cool in the pan for 10 minutes, then turn out and finish cooling on a wire rack. Cut into squares to serve.

**Serves 12**

* oil or melted butter, for greasing

scant 1 cup plumped pitted prunes

⅔ cup apple juice

1¾ cups all-purpose flour

2 tsp baking powder

* ¾ cup unsalted butter, softened

* generous ¾ cup superfine sugar

* 3 eggs, beaten

* 1 tsp vanilla extract

⅔ cup walnut pieces, coarsely chopped

# Coconut Lamingtons

1. Preheat the oven to 350°F/180°C. Grease and line a 9-inch/23-cm square cake pan.

2. Sift the flour and baking powder into a large bowl and add the butter, superfine sugar, eggs, and vanilla extract. Beat well until the mixture is smooth, then stir in the milk and coconut.

3. Spoon the mixture into the prepared pan and smooth the surface with a spatula. Bake in the preheated oven for 30–35 minutes, or until risen, firm, and golden brown.

4. Let cool in the pan for 10 minutes, then turn out and finish cooling on a wire rack. When the cake is cold, cut into 16 squares with a sharp knife.

5. For the icing, sift the confectioners' sugar and cocoa into a bowl. Add the water and butter and stir until smooth. Spread out the coconut on a large plate. Dip each piece of sponge cake into the icing, holding with 2 forks to coat evenly, then toss in coconut to cover.

6. Place on a sheet of parchment paper and let set.

**Makes 16**

* oil or melted butter, for greasing
* 1½ cups all-purpose flour
* 1 tbsp baking powder
* ¾ cup unsalted butter, softened
* generous ¾ cup superfine sugar
* 3 eggs, beaten
* 1 tsp vanilla extract
* 2 tbsp milk
  2 tbsp dry unsweetened coconut

**Icing and coating**
4½ cups confectioners' sugar
⅓ cup unsweetened cocoa
⅓ cup boiling water
5 tbsp unsalted butter, melted
3 cups dry unsweetened coconut

# Marshmallow Crunch Bars

1. Preheat the oven to 350°F/180°C. Grease and line a 9-inch/23-cm square cake pan.

2. Sift the flour and baking powder into a large bowl and add the butter, sugar, eggs, and vanilla extract. Beat well until the mixture is smooth. Stir about two-thirds of the nuts and candied cherries into the mixture.

3. Spoon the mixture into the prepared pan and smooth level with a spatula. Sprinkle the remaining nuts and candied cherries and the marshmallows over the top, pressing down lightly.

4. Bake in the preheated oven for 40–50 minutes, or until risen and golden brown.

5. Let cool in the pan for about 20 minutes, until firm, then cut into bars and finish cooling on a wire rack.

**Makes 8**

* oil or melted butter, for greasing
* 1½ cups all-purpose flour
* 1 tbsp baking powder
* ¾ cup unsalted butter, softened
* generous ¾ cup superfine sugar
* 3 eggs, beaten
* 1 tsp vanilla extract
  scant ½ cup chopped mixed nuts
  ⅓ cup candied cherries, coarsely chopped
  ½ cup mini marshmallows

# 20

# Cherry Almond Bars

1. Preheat the oven to 375°F/190°C. Grease and line a 7 x 11-inch/18 x 28-cm rectangular cake pan.

2. Sift the flour and baking powder into a bowl and add the butter, sugar, eggs, and almond extract. Stir in the lemon rind, ground almonds, and half the candied cherries.

3. Spoon the mixture into the prepared pan, smoothing level with a spatula. Sprinkle the remaining candied cherries and the slivered almonds over the mixture.

4. Bake in the preheated oven for 40–50 minutes, or until firm and golden brown. Let cool in the pan, then cut into bars to serve.

**Makes 8**

* oil or melted butter, for greasing
- 1 cup all-purpose flour
- 2 tsp baking powder
* ¾ cup unsalted butter, softened
* generous ¾ cup superfine sugar
* 3 eggs, beaten
* 1 tsp almond extract
- finely grated rind of 1 lemon
- 1 cup ground almonds
- ⅔ cup candied cherries, chopped
- ¼ cup slivered almonds

# Special

# 21

# White Chocolate Valentine's Gâteau

1. Preheat the oven to 325°F/160°C. Grease a 6¾-cup heart-shape cake pan.

2. Sift the flour and baking powder into a bowl and add the butter, sugar, eggs, and vanilla extract. Beat well until smooth, then stir in the grated chocolate.

3. Spoon the mixture into the prepared pan and spread the top level. Bake in the preheated oven for 45–55 minutes, or until risen, firm, and golden brown. Let cool in the pan for 10 minutes, then turn out onto a wire rack to finish cooling.

4. For the frosting, melt the chocolate with the milk in a heatproof bowl set over a pan of hot water. Remove from the heat and stir until smooth, then let cool for 10 minutes. Whip the cream until it holds soft peaks, then fold into the cooled chocolate mixture.

5. Sprinkle the cake with the rum, if using. Spread the frosting over the top and sides of the cake, swirling with a spatula, then decorate with candied violets.

**Serves 10**

* oil or melted butter, for greasing
* 1½ cups all-purpose flour
* 1 tbsp baking powder
* ¾ cup unsalted butter, softened
* generous ¾ cup superfine sugar
* 3 eggs, beaten
* 1 tsp vanilla extract
  ¼ cup grated white chocolate
  2 tbsp white rum (optional)
  candied violets, to decorate

**Frosting**
7 oz/200 g white chocolate
2 tbsp milk
scant 1 cup heavy cream

# 22

# Halloween Pumpkin Cake

1. Preheat the oven to 325°F/160°C. Grease and line a 9-inch/23-cm round, deep cake pan.

2. Sift the flour, baking powder, and pumpkin pie spice into a bowl and add the butter, sugar, eggs, and vanilla extract. Beat well until smooth, then stir in the pumpkin.

3. Spoon the mixture into the prepared pan and spread the top level. Bake in the preheated oven for 40–50 minutes, or until well risen, firm, and golden brown. Let cool in the pan for 10 minutes, then turn out onto a wire rack to finish cooling.

4. Brush the cake with the warmed apricot jelly. Knead orange food coloring into about three-quarters of the fondant and roll out to cover the top and sides of the cake. Trim the edges neatly, reserving the trimmings.

5. Form the trimmings into small pumpkin shapes, then use the black writing icing to pipe faces and the green writing icing to pipe stalks onto them. Knead black food coloring into the remaining fondant, then roll it out and cut into bat shapes. Pipe eyes onto the bats using yellow writing icing, then place the pumpkins and bats onto the cake to decorate.

**Serves 10**

* oil or melted butter, for greasing
* 1½ cups all-purpose flour
* 1 tbsp baking powder
  1 tsp pumpkin pie spice
* ¾ cup unsalted butter, softened
* generous ¾ cup light brown sugar
* 3 eggs, beaten
* 1 tsp vanilla extract
  1½ cups coarsely grated pumpkin flesh

**To decorate**
3 tbsp apricot jelly, warmed

a few drops of orange and black edible food colorings

1 lb 12 oz/800 g ready-to-roll fondant

black, green, and yellow writing icing

# Birthday Number Cake

1. Preheat the oven to 325°F/160°C. Grease and line a 10 x 7-inch/25 x 18-cm numeral cake pan or a frame on a cookie sheet, about 2 inches/5 cm deep.

2. Sift the flour and baking powder into a large bowl and add the butter, superfine sugar, eggs, and vanilla extract. Beat well until the mixture is smooth, then stir in the orange juice and rind.

3. Spoon the mixture into the prepared pan and smooth the surface with a spatula. Bake in the preheated oven for 40–50 minutes, or until risen, firm, and golden brown. Let cool in the pan for 5 minutes, then turn out and finish cooling on a wire rack.

4. For the frosting, beat together the confectioners' sugar, butter, orange rind, and juice until smooth. Spread over the cake evenly, smoothing with a spatula.

5. Arrange the orange slices on top of the cake to decorate, then add the birthday candles and serve.

**Serves 10–12**

- oil or melted butter, for greasing
- 1½ cups all-purpose flour
- 1 tbsp baking powder
- ¾ cup unsalted butter, softened
- generous ¾ cup superfine sugar
- 3 eggs, beaten
- 1 tsp vanilla extract
- 2 tbsp orange juice
  finely grated rind of ½ orange
  sugar orange slices and birthday candles, to decorate

**Frosting**
3 cups confectioners' sugar, sifted
¾ cup unsalted butter, softened
finely grated rind of ½ orange
1 tbsp orange juice

# Bumblebee Cake

1. Preheat the oven to 325°F/160°C. Grease a 6¾-cup heatproof bowl.

2. Sift the flour and baking powder into a bowl and add the butter, superfine sugar, eggs, and vanilla extract. Beat well until smooth, then stir in the lemon juice and rind.

3. Spoon the mixture into the prepared bowl and spread the top level. Bake in the preheated oven for 1¼–1½ hours, or until risen, firm, and golden brown. Let cool for 5 minutes in the bowl, then turn out onto a wire rack to finish cooling.

4. For the frosting, beat together the butter, confectioners' sugar, honey, and lemon juice until smooth. Slice the cake horizontally into 3 layers. Use about a quarter of the frosting to sandwich the cakes together.

5. Using a pastry bag fitted with a large plain tip, pipe the remaining frosting in lines around the cake to resemble a beehive.

6. Reserve a quarter of the white fondant, then color half the remainder yellow and half black. Shape to make small bees, making the wings from the white fondant and fixing with a dab of water. Press the bees into the frosting.

**Serves 8–10**

* oil or melted butter, for greasing

generous 2 cups all-purpose flour

* 1 tbsp baking powder
* ¾ cup unsalted butter, softened
* generous ¾ cup superfine sugar
* 3 eggs, beaten
* 1 tsp vanilla extract
* 2 tbsp lemon juice

finely grated rind of 1 lemon

**Frosting**
¾ cup unsalted butter
2¼ cups confectioners' sugar, sifted
3 tbsp honey
2 tbsp lemon juice

**To decorate**
9 oz/250 g white ready-to-roll fondant
a few drops of yellow and black edible food colorings

# Rich Chocolate Rum Torte

1. Preheat the oven to 350°F/180°C. Grease and line three 7-inch/18-cm layer cake pans.

2. Put the chocolate and milk into a small pan and heat gently, without boiling, until melted. Stir and remove from the heat.

3. Sift the flour and baking powder into a large bowl and add the butter, sugar, eggs, and vanilla extract. Beat well until smooth, then stir in the chocolate mixture.

4. Divide the mixture among the prepared pans and smooth the tops level. Bake in the preheated oven for 20–25 minutes, or until risen and firm to the touch.

5. Let cool in the pans for 5 minutes, then turn out and finish cooling on wire racks.

6. For the frosting, melt the chocolate with the cream and rum in a small pan over low heat. Remove from the heat and let cool, stirring occasionally, until it reaches a spreadable consistency.

7. Sandwich the cakes together with about a third of the frosting, then spread the remainder over the top and sides of the cake, swirling with a spatula. Sprinkle with chocolate curls or grated chocolate and let set.

**Serves 8**

* oil or melted butter, for greasing
* 2½ oz/70 g semisweet chocolate
* 2 tbsp milk
* 1½ cups all-purpose flour
* 1 tbsp baking powder
* ¾ cup unsalted butter, softened
* generous ¾ cup dark brown sugar
* 3 eggs, beaten
* 1 tsp vanilla extract
* chocolate curls or grated chocolate, to decorate

**Frosting**
8 oz/225 g semisweet chocolate
1 cup heavy cream
2 tbsp dark rum

# Orange Cheesecake Gâteau

1. Preheat the oven to 350°F/180°C. Grease and line two 9-inch/23-cm layer cake pans.

2. Sift the flour and baking powder into a large bowl and add the butter, superfine sugar, eggs, and orange flower water. Beat well until the mixture is smooth, then stir in the orange juice.

3. Divide the mixture between the prepared pans and smooth the surfaces with a spatula. Bake in the preheated oven for 25–30 minutes, or until risen and golden brown. Let cool in the pans for 5 minutes, then turn out and finish cooling on a wire rack.

4. Beat together all the frosting ingredients until smooth and spread about a third over one cake. Spoon the remainder into a pastry bag fitted with a large star tip and pipe swirls around the edge.

5. Place the second cake on top. Pipe the remaining frosting around the top edge. Fill the center with orange slices and brush with maple syrup.

**Serves 8–10**

* oil or melted butter, for greasing
* 1½ cups all-purpose flour
* 1 tbsp baking powder
* ¾ cup unsalted butter, softened
* generous ¾ cup superfine sugar
* 3 eggs, beaten
* 1 tsp orange flower water
* 2 tbsp orange juice

Frosting
2⅔ cups mascarpone cheese
finely grated rind of 1 orange
4 tbsp orange juice
½ cup confectioners' sugar
1 tsp orange flower water

Topping
1 orange, peeled and sliced
maple syrup, for brushing

# 27

# Polka-Dot Birthday Cake

1. Preheat the oven to 325°F/160°C. Grease and line two 8-inch/20 cm square layer cake pans.

2. Sift the flour and baking powder into a large bowl and add the butter, sugar, eggs, and vanilla extract. Beat well until the mixture is smooth, then stir in the milk.

3. Divide the mixture between the prepared pans and smooth the surfaces with a spatula. Bake in the preheated oven for 25–30 minutes, or until risen, firm, and golden brown. Let cool in the pans for 2–3 minutes, then turn out and finish cooling on a wire rack.

4. Warm the apricot jelly with the lemon juice in a small pan until melted. Spread half over one cake and place the other cake on top. Brush the remaining jelly over the top and sides of the cake.

5. Roll out the fondant to cover the cakes, smoothing with your hands, then trim the edges with a sharp knife. Decorate with candies and birthday candles.

**Serves 8–10**

* oil or melted butter, for greasing
* 1½ cups all-purpose flour
* 1 tbsp baking powder
* ¾ cup unsalted butter, softened
* generous ¾ cup superfine sugar
* 3 eggs, beaten
* 1 tsp vanilla extract
* 2 tbsp milk

  sugar-coated chocolate candies and birthday candles, to decorate

**Filling and topping**
5 tbsp apricot jelly
1 tbsp lemon juice
1 lb 2 oz/500 g ready-to-roll fondant

# 28

# Frosted Raspberry Almond Ring

1. Preheat the oven 325°F/160°C. Grease a 6¾-cup tube cake pan, preferably nonstick.

2. Sift the flour and baking powder into a large bowl and add the butter, superfine sugar, eggs, and almond extract. Beat well until the mixture is smooth, then stir in the ground almonds. Mash half the raspberries with a fork and stir into the mixture.

3. Spoon the mixture into the prepared pan and smooth the surface with a spatula. Bake in the preheated oven for 40–45 minutes, or until risen, firm, and golden brown.

4. Let cool in the pan for 10 minutes, then turn out carefully onto a wire rack to finish cooling.

5. For the frosting, place the egg white, confectioners' sugar, corn syrup, and cream of tartar in a bowl over a pan of hot water and whisk vigorously with an electric handheld mixer until thick enough to hold its shape.

6. Quickly swirl the frosting over the cake. Decorate with the remaining raspberries and the slivered almonds.

**Serves 8–10**

* oil or melted butter, for greasing
* 1½ cups all-purpose flour
* 1 tbsp baking powder
* ¾ cup unsalted butter, softened
* generous ¾ cup superfine sugar
* 3 eggs, beaten
* 1 tsp almond extract
  ⅔ cup ground almonds
  1⅓ cups fresh raspberries
  toasted slivered almonds, to decorate

**Frosting**
1 extra large egg white
1¼ cups confectioners' sugar
1 tbsp dark corn syrup
¼ tsp cream of tartar

# Glazed Fruit & Nut Cake

1. Preheat the oven to 325°F/160°C. Grease a 9-inch/23-cm round, springform cake pan and sprinkle with a little of the flour to coat, shaking out the excess.

2. Sift the flour, baking powder, and apple pie spice into a large bowl and add the butter, sugar, eggs, and vanilla extract. Beat well until the mixture is smooth, then stir in the milk, mixed dried fruit, and chopped nuts.

3. Spoon the mixture into the prepared pan and smooth the surface with a spatula. Bake in the preheated oven for about 1 hour, or until risen, firm, and golden brown.

4. Let cool in the pan for 30 minutes, then remove the sides and place on a wire rack to finish cooling.

5. Brush the top of the cake with a little of the warmed honey, then arrange the candied fruits and whole nuts on top. Brush with the remaining honey and let set.

**Serves 16–18**

- oil or melted butter, for greasing
- 2¼ cups all-purpose flour, plus extra for sprinkling
- 1 tbsp baking powder
- 1 tsp apple pie spice
- ¾ cup unsalted butter, softened
- generous ¾ cup dark brown sugar
- 3 eggs, beaten
- 1 tsp vanilla extract
- 2 tbsp milk
- 2 cups mixed dried fruit
- ¾ cup chopped mixed nuts

**To decorate**
- 3 tbsp honey, warmed
- 1½ cups mixed candied fruits, such as pineapple, cherries, and orange
- ½ cup whole shelled nuts, such as Brazil nuts, almonds, and walnuts

# Rose Gâteau

1. Preheat the oven to 350°F/180°C. Grease and line the bottoms of two 9-inch/23-cm layer cake pans.

2. Sift the flour and baking powder into a large bowl and add the butter, superfine sugar, eggs, and rose water. Beat well until the mixture is smooth, then stir in the milk.

3. Divide the mixture between the prepared pans and smooth the surfaces with a spatula. Bake in the preheated oven for 25–30 minutes, or until risen, firm, and golden brown. Let cool in the pans for 2–3 minutes, then turn out and finish cooling on a wire rack.

4. For the filling, whip the cream with ½ teaspoon of the rose water until just thick enough to hold its shape. Use to sandwich the cakes together.

5. For the icing, combine the confectioners' sugar with the remaining rose water and just enough water to mix to a thick pouring consistency. Spoon it over the cake, letting it drizzle down the sides. Let set.

6. Brush the rose petals with the egg white, sprinkle with superfine sugar, and arrange on top of the cake to decorate.

**Serves 8–10**

* oil or melted butter, for greasing
* 1½ cups all-purpose flour
* 1 tbsp baking powder
* ¾ cup unsalted butter, softened
* generous ¾ cup superfine sugar
* 3 eggs, beaten
* 1 tsp rose water
* 2 tbsp milk

**Filling and icing**
⅔ cup heavy cream
1 tsp rose water
1¾ cups confectioners' sugar, sifted

**To decorate**
fresh rose petals, washed and patted dry
½ egg white
superfine sugar, for sprinkling

# 31

# Christmas Mulled Sponge Loaf

1. Preheat the oven to 350°F/180°C. Grease and line a 5-cup loaf pan.

2. Sift the flour, baking powder, and apple pie spice into a large bowl and add the butter, brown sugar, eggs, and vanilla extract. Beat well until the mixture is smooth, then stir in the orange rind and juice.

3. Spoon the mixture into the prepared pan and smooth level with a spatula. Bake in the preheated oven for 40–50 minutes, or until risen, firm, and golden brown. (Don't worry if the cake dips slightly in the center.)

4. Remove the pan from the oven and stand it on a wire rack. To make the syrup, put the confectioners' sugar, port, and star anise into a pan and heat gently until boiling. Boil rapidly for 2–3 minutes to reduce slightly. Remove the star anise.

5. Spoon the syrup over the cake and let soak for 30 minutes. Turn out the cake from the pan, upside down.

6. Brush the cranberries and bay leaves with the egg white and sprinkle with the superfine sugar, then arrange on top of the cake.

**Serves 8**

* oil or melted butter, for greasing
* 1½ cups all-purpose flour
* 1 tbsp baking powder
  1 tsp apple pie spice
* ¾ cup unsalted butter, softened
* generous ¾ cup light brown sugar
* 3 eggs, beaten
* 1 tsp vanilla extract
  finely grated rind of 1 orange
* 2 tbsp orange juice

**Syrup**
⅔ cup confectioners' sugar
scant ½ cup port or red wine
1 piece of star anise

**To decorate**
10 fresh cranberries
10 fresh bay leaves
1 egg white
3 tbsp superfine sugar

# Silver Wedding Anniversary Cake

1. Preheat the oven to 350°F/180°C. Grease and line the bottoms of a 7-inch/18-cm layer cake pan and a 9-inch/ 23-cm layer cake pan.

2. Sift the flour and baking powder into a large bowl and add the butter, superfine sugar, eggs, and vanilla extract. Beat well until the mixture is smooth, then stir in the milk.

3. Spoon the mixture into the prepared pans and smooth the surfaces with a spatula. Bake in the preheated oven for 20–25 minutes for the small cake and 25–30 minutes for the large cake, or until risen, firm, and golden brown.

4. Cool the cakes in the pans for 2–3 minutes, then turn out and finish cooling on wire racks. Prick the cakes with a skewer and sprinkle with sherry.

5. For the frosting, beat together the mascarpone, cream, and confectioners' sugar to a smooth, spreading consistency, adding a little more confectioners' sugar if needed. Spread a little frosting on top of the center of the larger cake, then place the small cake on top, pressing down lightly.

6. Spread the remaining frosting over the cakes, swirling with a spatula, then decorate with silver balls.

**Serves 10–12**

* oil or melted butter, for greasing
* 1½ cups all-purpose flour
* 1 tbsp baking powder
* ¾ cup unsalted butter, softened
* generous ¾ cup superfine sugar
* 3 eggs, beaten
* 1 tsp vanilla extract
* 2 tbsp milk
  2 tbsp medium sherry
  silver balls, to decorate

Frosting
generous 1 cup mascarpone cheese
3 tbsp light cream
2¼ cups confectioners' sugar, sifted, plus extra if needed

# Easter Cake

1. Preheat the oven to 325°F/160°C. Grease and line a 9-inch/23-cm square cake pan.

2. Sift the flour, baking powder, and apple pie spice into a large bowl and add the butter, sugar, eggs, and almond extract. Beat well until the mixture is smooth, then stir in the milk, ground almonds, and mixed dried fruit.

3. Spoon the mixture into the prepared pan and smooth the surface with a spatula. Bake in the preheated oven for 1–1¼ hours, or until risen, firm, and golden brown. Let cool in the pan for 30 minutes, then turn out onto a wire rack to finish cooling.

4. Brush the top of the cake the warmed apricot jelly. Roll out about half the marzipan and use to cover the top of the cake, trimming the edges neatly. Score the top lightly with a knife in a diamond pattern.

5. Roll the remaining marzipan into 12 thin ropes, each about 10 inches/25 cm long, and braid together in threes. Arrange 1 braid along each top edge of the cake, trimming the ends.

6. Preheat the broiler to high. Lightly brush the marzipan with the egg white, then broil the cake for 3–4 minutes, or until golden brown on top. Let cool before serving.

**Serves 16**

- oil or melted butter, for greasing
- 2 cups all-purpose flour
- 2½ tsp baking powder
- 1 tsp apple pie spice
- ¾ cup unsalted butter, softened
- generous ¾ cup light brown sugar
- 3 eggs, beaten
- 1 tsp almond extract
- 2 tbsp milk
- ¾ cup ground almonds
- generous 2⅓ cups mixed dried fruit

**To decorate**
- 2 tbsp apricot jelly, warmed
- 2 lb/900 g golden marzipan
- egg white, for brushing

# 34

# Walnut Torte

1. Preheat the oven to 350°F/180°C. Grease and line the bottoms of two 8-inch/20-cm layer cake pans.

2. Sift the flour and baking powder into a large bowl and add the butter, superfine sugar, eggs, and vanilla extract. Beat well until the mixture is smooth, then stir in the milk and ⅓ cup of the chopped walnuts.

3. Divide the mixture between the prepared pans and smooth the surfaces with a spatula. Bake in the preheated oven for 25–30 minutes, or until risen, firm, and golden brown.

4. Let cool in the pans for 2–3 minutes, then turn out and finish cooling on a wire rack. Slice each cake in half horizontally to make 4 layers in total.

5. For the frosting, beat together the butter, confectioners' sugar, and cream until smooth. Spread about half the frosting over the top of 3 of the cakes and sandwich them together, placing the plain one on top.

6. Spread half the remaining frosting over the sides of the cake to cover thinly and press the remaining chopped walnuts over it. Brush the apricot jelly over the top of the cake. Spoon the remaining frosting into a pastry bag fitted with a star tip and pipe swirls of frosting around the top edge of the cake. Decorate the top with walnut halves.

**Serves 8–10**

* oil or melted butter, for greasing
* 1½ cups all-purpose flour
* 1 tbsp baking powder
* ¾ cup unsalted butter, softened
* generous ¾ cup superfine sugar
* 3 eggs, beaten
* 1 tsp vanilla extract
* 2 tbsp milk
  generous 1 cup finely chopped walnuts
  3 tbsp apricot jelly, warmed
  walnut halves, to decorate

**Frosting**
¾ cup unsalted butter, softened
3 cups confectioners' sugar, sifted
scant ½ cup light cream

# Meringue-Topped Coffee Liqueur Cake

1. Preheat the oven to 325°F/160°C. Grease and line a 10-inch/25-cm round cake pan.

2. Sift the flour and baking powder into a large bowl and add the butter, brown sugar, eggs, and coffee extract. Beat well until the mixture is smooth, then stir in the milk.

3. Spoon the mixture into the prepared pan and smooth the surface with a spatula. Bake in the preheated oven for 40–50 minutes, or until risen, firm, and golden brown.

4. Let cool in the pan for 2–3 minutes, then turn out onto a flameproof serving plate. Prick the cake all over with a skewer, then sprinkle with the liqueur.

5. For the meringue topping, put the egg whites into a clean bowl and whisk with an electric handheld mixer until thick enough to hold soft peaks. Gradually add the superfine sugar, whisking vigorously after each addition, then whisk in the coffee extract.

6. Spoon the meringue on top of the cake and spread into peaks and swirls with a spatula. Use a chef's blowtorch to brown the meringue, or place the cake under a hot broiler for 2–3 minutes, or until just browned but still soft inside. Cut into slices and serve.

**Serves 6–8**

* oil or melted butter, for greasing
* 1½ cups all-purpose flour
* 1 tbsp baking powder
* ¾ cup unsalted butter, softened
* generous ¾ cup light brown sugar
* 3 eggs, beaten
* 1 tsp coffee extract
* 2 tbsp milk
  3 tbsp coffee liqueur

**Meringue topping**
3 egg whites
¾ cup superfine sugar
1½ tsp coffee extract

# Strawberry Mousse Cake

1. Preheat the oven to 325°F/160°C. Grease and line a 9-inch/23 cm round, springform cake pan.

2. Sift the flour and baking powder into a large bowl and add the butter, sugar, eggs, and vanilla extract. Beat well until the mixture is smooth, then stir in the milk.

3. Spoon the mixture into the prepared pan and smooth the surface with a spatula. Bake in the preheated oven for 45–55 minutes, or until risen and golden brown.

4. Let cool in the pan for 5 minutes, then turn out and finish cooling on a wire rack. Cut the cake in half horizontally and place half back in the cake pan.

5. For the filling, dissolve the gelatin in the orange juice in a small bowl placed in a pan of hot water. In a blender or processor, puree 3½ cups of the strawberries with the sugar. Whip the cream until thick enough to hold its shape. Quickly stir the gelatin into the strawberry mixture, then fold in the cream.

6. Pour the mixture into the pan and place the second half of cake on top. Chill in the refrigerator until set. Turn out the cake and spread the top with warmed grape jelly. Decorate with the remaining strawberries.

## Serves 8–10

* oil or melted butter, for greasing
* 1½ cups all-purpose flour
* 1 tbsp baking powder
* ¾ cup unsalted butter, softened
* generous ¾ cup superfine sugar
* 3 eggs, beaten
* 1 tsp vanilla extract
* 2 tbsp milk

### Filling and topping
4 tsp powdered gelatin
3 tbsp orange juice
5 cups fresh strawberries
3 tbsp superfine sugar
1½ cups heavy cream
scant ½ cup grape jelly, warmed

# 37

# Lemon & Pistachio Ring

1. Preheat the oven to 350°F/180°C. Grease a 6¾-cup Bundt cake pan.

2. Sift the flour and baking powder into a large bowl and add the butter, sugar, eggs, and lemon extract. Beat well until the mixture is smooth, then stir in the lemon rind, lemon juice, and finely chopped pistachios.

3. Spoon the mixture into the prepared pan and smooth the surface with a spatula. Bake in the preheated oven for 40–50 minutes, or until risen, firm, and golden brown.

4. Let cool in the pan for 10 minutes, then turn out onto a wire rack to finish cooling.

5. To decorate, thinly pare the zest from the lemon. Cut into long, thin strips and place in a pan with the sugar and water. Heat gently until the sugar dissolves, then bring to a boil and boil for 7 minutes. Remove the strips of zest from the syrup and let cool on a sheet of parchment paper.

6. Arrange the candied lemon strips on top of the cake and sprinkle with coarsely chopped pistachios.

**Serves 10**

* oil or melted butter, for greasing
* 1½ cups all-purpose flour
  2 tsp baking powder
* ¾ cup unsalted butter, softened
* generous ¾ cup superfine sugar
* 3 eggs, beaten
* 1 tsp lemon extract
  finely grated rind of 1 lemon
  1 tbsp lemon juice
  ⅓ cup finely chopped pistachios

**To decorate**
1 lemon
scant ½ cup superfine sugar
¼ cup water
2 tbsp coarsely chopped pistachios

# 38

# Blueberry Swirl Gâteau

1. Preheat the oven to 325°F/160°C. Grease and line the bottoms of three 7½-inch/19-cm layer cake pans.

2. Sift the flour and baking powder into a large bowl and add the butter, superfine sugar, eggs, and orange flower water. Beat well until the mixture is smooth, then stir in the orange juice.

3. Divide the mixture among the prepared pans and smooth the surfaces with a spatula. Bake in the preheated oven for 20–25 minutes, or until risen, firm, and golden brown.

4. Let cool in the pans for 2–3 minutes, then turn out and finish cooling on a wire rack.

5. For the frosting, beat together the cream cheese and confectioners' sugar until smooth. Transfer about two-thirds of the mixture to a separate bowl and stir in 1¼ cups of the blueberries, then use this to sandwich the cakes together.

6. Rub the remaining blueberries through a fine mesh strainer to make a smooth puree. Spread the remaining frosting on top of the cake and swirl the blueberry puree through it.

## Serves 8–10

* oil or melted butter, for greasing
* 1½ cups all-purpose flour
* 1 tbsp baking powder
* ¾ cup unsalted butter, softened
* generous ¾ cup superfine sugar
* 3 eggs, beaten
* 1 tsp orange flower water
* 2 tbsp orange juice

**Frosting and filling**
scant 1 cup whole-fat cream cheese
scant 1 cup confectioners' sugar, sifted
2 cups fresh blueberries

# Caramel Sponge Layer

1. Preheat the oven to 350°F/180°C. Grease and line a 9-inch/23-cm square cake pan.

2. Sift the flour and baking powder into a large bowl and add the butter, brown sugar, eggs, and vanilla extract. Beat well until the mixture is smooth, then stir in the milk.

3. Spoon into the prepared pan and smooth the surface level. Bake in the preheated oven for 35–40 minutes, or until risen, firm, and golden brown.

4. Let cool in the pan for 5 minutes, then turn out and finish cooling on a wire rack. Slice the cake horizontally into 2 layers.

5. For the frosting, heat the corn syrup in a pan until very hot. Gradually pour into the egg yolks, whisking vigorously until the mixture is pale and thick. Whisk in the butter and vanilla extract to make a glossy frosting. Cover and let cool.

6. Heat the superfine sugar in a heavy pan over low heat until melted. Boil to a rich, golden caramel. Immediately pour onto a greased cookie sheet. Let set.

7. Crush half the caramel finely, then stir into half the frosting and use to sandwich the cakes together. Spread the remaining frosting on top. Break the remaining caramel into small pieces, then scatter on top of the cake to decorate.

**Serves 10–12**

* oil or melted butter, for greasing
* 1½ cups all-purpose flour
* 1 tbsp baking powder
* ¾ cup unsalted butter, softened
* generous ¾ cup light brown sugar
* 3 eggs, beaten
* 1 tsp vanilla extract
* 2 tbsp milk

**Frosting and decoration**
⅓ cup dark corn syrup
2 egg yolks, beaten
¾ cup unsalted butter, softened
1 tsp vanilla extract
generous ¾ cup superfine sugar

# Marbled Pastel Cake

1. Preheat the oven to 325°F/160°C. Grease and line a 9-inch/23-cm round, deep cake pan.

2. Sift the flour and baking powder into a large bowl and add the butter, sugar, eggs, and vanilla extract. Beat well until the mixture is smooth, then stir in the milk. Spoon half the mixture into a separate bowl and stir in a few drops of food coloring.

3. Spoon alternate tablespoonfuls of the two mixtures into the prepared pan and swirl lightly with a spatula for a marbled effect.

4. Bake in the preheated oven for 40–50 minutes, or until risen, firm, and golden brown. Let cool in the pan for 10 minutes, then turn out and finish cooling on a wire rack.

5. Divide the fondant in half and knead a few drops of food coloring into one half. Place the white and pink mixtures together and knead together for a marbled effect.

6. Place the cake on a board, brush with apricot jelly, and roll out the fondant to cover the cake. Trim the edges, then roll the trimmings into 2 long ropes, twist together, and place around the bottom of the cake. Decorate with sugar flowers.

## Serves 12

* oil or melted butter, for greasing
* 1½ cups all-purpose flour
* 1 tbsp baking powder
* ¾ cup unsalted butter, softened
* generous ¾ cup superfine sugar
* 3 eggs, beaten
* 1 tsp vanilla extract
* 2 tbsp milk
  pink edible food coloring
  1 lb 9 oz/700 g ready-to-roll fondant
  3 tbsp apricot jelly, warmed
  sugar flowers, to decorate

# Dainty

# 41

# Vanilla Hazelnut Yogurt Cupcakes

1. Preheat the oven to 375°F/190°C. Put 26 paper liners into shallow muffin pans or put double-layer liners onto cookie sheets.

2. Sift the flour, cornstarch, and baking powder into a large bowl and add the yogurt, sugar, eggs, and vanilla extract. Beat well until the mixture is smooth, then stir in the finely chopped hazelnuts.

3. Divide the mixture among the paper liners. Bake in the preheated oven for 15–20 minutes, or until risen, firm, and golden brown. Transfer the cupcakes to a wire rack to cool.

4. For the topping, combine the confectioners' sugar and yogurt until smooth, then drizzle the mixture over the cupcakes. Sprinkle with the coarsely chopped hazelnuts and let set.

**Makes 26**

* 1½ cups all-purpose flour
  2 tsp cornstarch
* 1 tbsp baking powder
* ¾ cup plain yogurt
* generous ¾ cup superfine sugar
* 3 eggs, beaten
* 1 tsp vanilla extract
  ⅓ cup finely chopped hazelnuts

**Topping**
scant 1 cup confectioners' sugar, sifted
3 tbsp plain yogurt
⅓ cup coarsely chopped hazelnuts

# 42

# Almond & Apricot Spice Cupcakes

1. Preheat the oven to 375°F/190°C. Put 30 paper liners into shallow muffin pans or put double-layer liners onto cookie sheets.

2. Sift the flour, baking powder, and allspice into a large bowl and add the butter, sugar, eggs, and almond extract. Beat well until the mixture is smooth, then stir in the milk, apricots, and ground almonds.

3. Divide the mixture among the paper liners. Bake in the preheated oven for 15–20 minutes, or until risen, firm, and golden brown. Transfer the cupcakes to a wire rack to cool.

4. Spoon about a teaspoonful of the dulce de leche on top of each cupcake, then top with the slivered almonds.

**Makes 30**

* 1½ cups all-purpose flour
* 1 tbsp baking powder
  1 tsp ground allspice
* ¾ cup unsalted butter, softened
* generous ¾ cup superfine sugar
* 3 eggs, beaten
* 1 tsp almond extract
* 2 tbsp milk
  ⅓ cup finely chopped plumped dried apricots
  ⅓ cup ground almonds
  generous ⅔ cup dulce de leche
  ¼ cup toasted slivered almonds

# 43

# Maple Pecan Cupcakes

1. Preheat the oven to 375°F/190°C. Put 30 paper liners into shallow muffin pans or put double-layer liners onto cookie sheets.

2. Sift the flour and baking powder into a large bowl and add the butter, sugar, maple syrup, eggs, and vanilla extract. Beat well until the mixture is smooth, then stir in the pecans.

3. Divide the mixture among the paper liners. For the topping, combine the pecans, flour, sugar, and melted butter to make a crumbly mixture and spoon a little on top of each cake.

4. Bake in the preheated oven for 15–20 minutes, or until risen, firm, and golden brown. Transfer the cupcakes to a wire rack to cool.

**Makes 30**

* 1½ cups all-purpose flour
* 1 tbsp baking powder
* ¾ cup unsalted butter, softened
  generous ½ cup light brown sugar
  4 tbsp maple syrup
* 3 eggs, beaten
* 1 tsp vanilla extract
  ¼ cups finely chopped pecans

**Topping**
⅓ cup finely chopped pecans
2 tbsp all-purpose flour
2 tbsp light brown sugar
2 tbsp melted butter

# 44

# Cherry Cupcakes with Ricotta Frosting

**1** Preheat the oven to 375°F/190°C. Put 28 paper liners into shallow muffin pans or put double-layer liners onto cookie sheets.

**2** Stir a tablespoon of the flour into the cherries. Sift the remaining flour with the baking powder and cornstarch into a large bowl and add the butter, superfine sugar, eggs, and vanilla extract. Beat well until the mixture is smooth, then stir in the cherries.

**3** Divide the mixture among the paper liners. Bake in the preheated oven for 15–20 minutes, or until risen, firm, and golden brown. Transfer the cupcakes to a wire rack to cool.

**4** For the frosting, combine the ricotta, confectioners' sugar, and vanilla extract, then spoon a little on top of each cupcake. Top each with half a candied cherry.

**Makes 28**

✳ 1½ cups all-purpose flour

⅓ cup candied cherries, chopped

✳ 1 tbsp baking powder

1 tbsp cornstarch

✳ ¾ cup unsalted butter, softened

✳ generous ¾ cup superfine sugar

✳ 3 eggs, beaten

✳ 1 tsp vanilla extract

14 candied cherries, halved, to decorate

**Frosting**

generous 1 cup ricotta cheese

⅔ cup confectioners' sugar

½ tsp vanilla extract

# 45

# White Chocolate Chip Cupcakes

1. Preheat the oven to 375°F/190°C. Put 32 paper liners into shallow muffin pans or put double-layer liners onto cookie sheets.

2. Sift the flour and baking powder into a large bowl and add the butter, sugar, eggs, and vanilla extract. Beat well until the mixture is smooth, then stir in half the chocolate chips.

3. Divide the mixture among the paper liners and sprinkle with the remaining chocolate chips. Bake in the preheated oven for 15–20 minutes, or until risen, firm, and golden brown. Transfer the cupcakes to a wire rack to cool.

4. When the cupcakes are cold, spoon a little melted white chocolate on top of each and decorate with the chocolate sprinkles. Let set.

**Makes 32**

* 1½ cups all-purpose flour
* 1 tbsp baking powder
* ¾ cup unsalted butter, softened
* generous ¾ cup superfine sugar
* 3 eggs, beaten
* 1 tsp vanilla extract
  scant ½ cup white chocolate chips

**Topping**
3½ oz/100 g white chocolate, melted
2 tbsp chocolate sprinkles

# Fairy Flyaway Cupcakes

1. Preheat the oven to 375°F/190°C. Put 28 paper liners into shallow muffin pans or put double-layer liners onto cookie sheets.

2. Sift the flour and baking powder into a large bowl and add the butter, superfine sugar, eggs, and vanilla extract. Beat well until the mixture is smooth, then stir in enough of the milk to make a pourable consistency.

3. Divide the mixture among the paper liners. Bake in the preheated oven for 15–20 minutes, or until risen, firm, and golden brown. Transfer the cupcakes to a wire rack to cool.

4. For the buttercream, beat together the butter, confectioners' sugar, and vanilla extract until smooth.

5. Use a serrated knife to cut a round from the top of each cake, then cut each round in half. Spread or pipe a little of the buttercream on top of each cake, then press the pieces of cake into it to resemble butterfly wings. Decorate with the colored sprinkles.

**Makes 28**

* 1½ cups all-purpose flour
* 1 tbsp baking powder
* ¾ cup unsalted butter, softened
* generous ¾ cup superfine sugar
* 3 eggs, beaten
* 1 tsp vanilla extract
  1–2 tbsp milk
  colored sprinkles, to decorate

**Buttercream**
scant ½ cup unsalted butter, softened
1¾ cups confectioners' sugar
½ tsp vanilla extract

# Raspberry Ripple Cupcakes

1. Preheat the oven to 375°F/190°C. Put 32 paper liners into shallow muffin pans or put double-layer liners onto cookie sheets.

2. Sift the flour, baking powder, and cornstarch into a large bowl and add the butter, sugar, eggs, and almond extract. Beat well until the mixture is smooth. Mash the raspberries lightly with a fork, then fold into the mix.

3. Divide the mixture among the paper liners. Bake in the preheated oven for 15–20 minutes, or until risen, firm, and golden brown. Transfer the cupcakes to a wire rack to cool.

4. Sprinkle with vanilla sugar before serving.

**Makes 32**

* 1½ cups all-purpose flour
* 1 tbsp baking powder
  1 tbsp cornstarch
* ¾ cup unsalted butter, softened
* generous ¾ cup superfine sugar
* 3 eggs, beaten
* 1 tsp almond extract
  generous 1 cup fresh raspberries
  vanilla sugar, for sprinkling

# 48

# Banana Passion Fruit Cupcakes

1. Preheat the oven to 375°F/190°C. Put 30 paper liners into shallow muffin pans or put double-layer liners onto cookie sheets.

2. Sift the flour, baking powder, and cornstarch into a large bowl and add the butter, sugar, eggs, and vanilla extract. Beat well until the mixture is smooth. Mash 1 of the bananas with 1 tablespoon of the lemon juice and stir into the mix.

3. Divide the mixture among the paper liners and bake in the preheated oven for 15–20 minutes, or until risen, firm, and golden brown. Transfer the cupcakes to a wire rack to cool.

4. Halve the passion fruit and scoop out the pulp into a small bowl, then stir in the honey. Thinly slice the remaining banana and brush with the remaining lemon juice. Place a banana slice on top of each cupcake and spread a little of the passion fruit glaze over the top.

**Makes 30**

※ 1½ cups all-purpose flour
※ 1 tbsp baking powder
1 tbsp cornstarch
※ ¾ cup unsalted butter, softened
※ generous ¾ cup light brown sugar
※ 3 eggs, beaten
※ 1 tsp vanilla extract
2 ripe bananas
2 tbsp lemon juice
2 passion fruit
2 tbsp honey

# Christmas Cupcakes

1. Preheat the oven to 375°F/190°C. Put 36 paper liners into shallow muffin pans or put double-layer liners onto cookie sheets.

2. Sift the flour, baking powder, and cinnamon into a large bowl and add the butter, sugar, eggs, and almond extract. Beat well until the mixture is smooth, then stir in the sherry, orange rind, ground almonds, and mixed dried fruit.

3. Divide the mixture among the paper liners. Bake in the preheated oven for 15–20 minutes, or until risen, firm, and golden brown. Transfer the cupcakes to a wire rack to cool.

4. To decorate, roll out about three-quarters of the white fondant thinly and cut into 2-inch/5-cm rounds. Brush with a little water and fix one on top of each cupcake.

5. Color three-quarters of the remaining fondant green and color the remainder red. Roll out the green fondant and use a small cutter to cut out holly leaves, then shape tiny balls from the red fondant to resemble berries.

6. Brush the leaves and berries with a little water, then attach on top of the cupcakes and let dry.

**Makes 36**

* 1½ cups all-purpose flour
* 1 tbsp baking powder
  1 tsp ground cinnamon
* ¾ cup unsalted butter, softened
* generous ¾ cup light brown sugar
* 3 eggs, beaten
* 1 tsp almond extract
  2 tbsp medium sherry
  1 tbsp finely grated orange rind
  2 tbsp ground almonds
  ⅓ cup mixed dried fruit

**To decorate**
1 lb/450 g white ready-to-roll fondant
a few drops of green and red edible food coloring

# Blueberry Cupcakes with Sour Cream Frosting

1. Preheat the oven to 375°F/190°C. Put 30 paper liners into shallow muffin pans or put double-layer liners onto cookie sheets.

2. Sift the flour and baking powder into a large bowl and add the butter, superfine sugar, eggs, and vanilla extract. Beat well until the mixture is smooth. Add the orange rind and scant 1 cup of the blueberries.

3. Divide the mixture among the paper liners. Bake in the preheated oven for 15–20 minutes, or until risen, firm, and golden brown. Transfer the cupcakes to a wire rack to cool.

4. For the frosting, stir the sour cream into the confectioners' sugar and mix well until smooth. Spoon a little on top of each cupcake and top with the remaining blueberries. Let set.

**Makes 30**

* 1½ cups all-purpose flour
* 1 tbsp baking powder
* ¾ cup unsalted butter, softened
* generous ¾ cup superfine sugar
* 3 eggs, beaten
* 1 tsp vanilla extract
  finely grated rind of ½ orange
  1⅓ cups fresh blueberries

**Frosting**
3 tbsp sour cream
1⅓ cups confectioners' sugar, sifted

# 51

# Butterscotch Cupcakes

1. Preheat the oven to 375°F/190°C. Put 28 paper liners into shallow muffin pans or put double-layer liners onto cookie sheets.

2. Sift the flour and baking powder into a large bowl and add the butter, sugar, eggs, and vanilla extract. Beat well until the mixture is smooth.

3. Divide the mixture among the paper liners. Bake in the preheated oven for 15–20 minutes, or until risen, firm, and golden brown. Transfer the cupcakes to a wire rack to cool.

4. For the topping, put the corn syrup, butter, and sugar into a small pan and heat gently, stirring, until the sugar dissolves. Bring to a boil and cook, stirring, for about 1 minute. Drizzle the mixture over the cupcakes and let set.

**Makes 28**

* 1½ cups all-purpose flour
* 1 tbsp baking powder
* ¾ cup unsalted butter, softened
* generous ¾ cup light brown sugar
* 3 eggs, beaten
* 1 tsp vanilla extract

**Topping**
2 tbsp dark corn syrup
2 tbsp unsalted butter
2 tbsp dark brown sugar

# 52

# Teatime Cupcakes

1. Preheat the oven to 350°F/180°C. Put 10 ovenproof teacups (about the same size as a 1-cup measuring cup) onto cookie sheets.

2. Sift the flour, baking powder, and apple pie spice into a large bowl and add the butter, superfine sugar, eggs, and vanilla extract. Beat well until the mixture is smooth, then stir in the tea and half the currants.

3. Divide the mixture among the cups and sprinkle with the remaining currants. Bake in the preheated oven for 20–25 minutes, or until risen, firm, and golden brown. Turn out the cupcakes onto a wire rack to cool.

4. To serve, dust the cupcakes with a little confectioners' sugar and apple pie spice.

**Makes 10**

- 1½ cups all-purpose flour
- 1 tbsp baking powder
- ½ tsp apple pie spice
- ¾ cup unsalted butter, softened
- generous ¾ cup superfine sugar
- 3 eggs, beaten
- 1 tsp vanilla extract
- 2 tbsp strong Earl Grey tea
- ¼ cup currants
- confectioners' sugar and apple pie spice, for dusting

# 53

# Jelly Cupcakes

1. Preheat the oven to 375°F/190°C. Put 28 paper liners into shallow muffin pans or put double-layer liners onto cookie sheets.

2. Sift the flour, baking powder, and cornstarch into a large bowl and add the butter, superfine sugar, eggs, and vanilla extract. Beat well until the mixture is smooth.

3. Divide the mixture among the paper liners and put about ½ teaspoon jelly onto the center of each, without pressing down.

4. Bake in the preheated oven for 15–20 minutes, or until risen, firm, and golden brown. Transfer the cupcakes to a wire rack to cool. Dust with confectioners' sugar before serving.

**Makes 28**

* 1½ cups all-purpose flour
* 1 tbsp baking powder
  1 tbsp cornstarch
* ¾ cup unsalted butter, softened
* generous ¾ cup superfine sugar
* 3 eggs, beaten
* 1 tsp vanilla extract
  ¼ cup raspberry jelly
  confectioners' sugar, for dusting

# 54

# Orange Saffron Mini Cupcakes

1. Preheat the oven to 375°F/190°C. Arrange 90 mini paper liners on 2–3 cookie sheets.

2. Heat 2 tablespoons of the orange juice with the saffron until almost boiling, then remove from the heat and let stand for 10 minutes.

3. Sift the flour and baking powder into a large bowl and add the butter, superfine sugar, and eggs. Beat well until the mixture is smooth, then stir in the orange rind and half the saffron-and-orange juice mixture.

4. Divide the mixture among the paper liners. Bake in the preheated oven for 12–15 minutes, or until risen, firm, and golden brown. Transfer the cupcakes to a wire rack to cool.

5. Combine the remaining saffron-and-orange juice mixture and the confectioners' sugar to make a smooth paste, adding a little extra orange juice if needed. Spoon a little on top of each cake, top with strips of orange zest, and let set.

**Makes 90**

2–3 tbsp orange juice
pinch of saffron threads
❋ 1½ cups all-purpose flour
❋ 1 tbsp baking powder
❋ ¾ cup unsalted butter, softened
❋ generous ¾ cup superfine sugar
❋ 3 eggs, beaten
finely grated rind of 1 orange

**Topping**
1⅓ cups confectioners' sugar, sifted
fine strips of orange zest

# Flaky Chocolate Cupcakes

1. Preheat the oven to 375°F/190°C. Put 30 paper liners into shallow muffin pans or put double-layer liners onto cookie sheets.

2. Sift the flour and baking powder into a large bowl and add the butter, sugar, eggs, and vanilla extract. Beat well until the mixture is smooth. Combine the milk and cocoa and stir into the mix.

3. Divide the mixture among the paper liners and sprinkle with about a quarter of the crumbled chocolate. Bake in the preheated oven for 15–20 minutes, or until risen, firm, and golden brown. Transfer the cupcakes to a wire rack to cool.

4. When the cupcakes are cold, brush the tops with the apricot jelly and sprinkle with the remaining crumbled chocolate.

**Makes 30**

* 1½ cups all-purpose flour
* 1 tbsp baking powder
* ¾ cup unsalted butter, softened
* generous ¾ cup superfine sugar
* 3 eggs, beaten
* 1 tsp vanilla extract
* 2 tbsp milk
  1 tbsp unsweetened cocoa
  2½ oz/70 g flaky chocolate, crumbled
  3 tbsp apricot jelly, warmed

# 56

# Chocolate Honeycomb Cupcakes

1  Preheat the oven to 375°F/190°C. Put 30 paper liners into shallow muffin pans or put double-layer liners onto cookie sheets.

2  Sift the flour and baking powder into a large bowl and add the butter, superfine sugar, eggs, and vanilla extract. Beat well until the mixture is smooth, then stir in the chopped honeycomb.

3  Divide the mixture among the paper liners. Bake in the preheated oven for 15–20 minutes, or until risen, firm, and golden brown. Transfer the cupcakes to a wire rack to cool.

4  For the topping, combine the confectioners' sugar, cocoa, and water into a smooth paste. Spoon a little on top of each cupcake and top with chunks of honeycomb. Let set.

**Makes 30**

* 1½ cups all-purpose flour
* 1 tbsp baking powder
* ¾ cup unsalted butter, softened
* generous ¾ cup superfine sugar
* 3 eggs, beaten
* 1 tsp vanilla extract
    1½ oz/40 g chocolate-covered honeycomb, finely chopped

**Topping**

1¾ cups confectioners' sugar, sifted

2 tsp unsweetened cocoa

about 2 tbsp water

1½ oz/40 g chocolate-covered honeycomb, cut into chunks

# 57

# Coffee Fudge Cupcakes

1. Preheat the oven to 375°F/190°C. Put 28 paper liners into shallow muffin pans or put double-layer liners onto cookie sheets.

2. Sift the flour and baking powder into a large bowl and add the butter, superfine sugar, eggs, and coffee extract. Beat well until the mixture is smooth, then beat in the milk.

3. Divide the mixture among the paper liners. Bake in the preheated oven for 15–20 minutes, or until risen, firm, and golden brown. Transfer the cupcakes to a wire rack to cool.

4. For the frosting, put the butter, brown sugar, cream, and coffee extract into a pan over medium heat and stir until smooth. Bring to a boil and boil for 2 minutes, stirring. Remove from the heat and beat in the confectioners' sugar.

5. Stir until smooth and thick, then spoon into a pastry bag fitted with a large star tip. Pipe a swirl of frosting on top of each cupcake and top with a coffee bean.

## Makes 28

* 1½ cups all-purpose flour
* 1 tbsp baking powder
* ¾ cup unsalted butter, softened
* generous ¾ cup superfine sugar
* 3 eggs, beaten
* 1 tsp coffee extract
* 2 tbsp milk
  chocolate-covered coffee beans, to decorate

### Frosting
¼ cup unsalted butter

generous ½ cup light brown sugar

2 tbsp light cream or milk

½ tsp coffee extract

3½ cups confectioners' sugar, sifted

# 58

# Gingerbread Cupcakes

1. Preheat the oven to 375°F/190°C. Put 30 paper liners into shallow muffin pans or put double-layer liners onto cookie sheets.

2. Sift the flour, baking powder, ginger, and cinnamon into a large bowl and add the butter, sugar, eggs, and vanilla extract. Beat well until the mixture is smooth.

3. Divide the mixture among the paper liners. Bake in the preheated oven for 15–20 minutes, or until risen, firm, and golden brown. Transfer the cupcakes to a wire rack cool.

4. For the frosting, beat together the butter, confectioners' sugar, and orange juice until smooth. Spoon a little frosting on top of each cupcake and top with candied ginger.

**Makes 30**

- 1½ cups all-purpose flour
- 1 tbsp baking powder
- 2 tsp ground ginger
- 1 tsp ground cinnamon
- ¾ cup unsalted butter, softened
- generous ¾ cup dark brown sugar
- 3 eggs, beaten
- 1 tsp vanilla extract
- chopped candied ginger, to decorate

Frosting
- 6 tbsp unsalted butter, softened
- 1⅓ cups confectioners' sugar, sifted
- 3 tbsp orange juice

# 59

# Peppermint Chocolate Chip Cupcakes

1. Preheat the oven to 375°F/190°C. Put 32 paper liners into shallow muffin pans or put double-layer liners onto cookie sheets.

2. Sift the flour and baking powder into a large bowl and add the butter, sugar, eggs, and peppermint extract. Beat well until the mixture is smooth, then stir in half the chocolate chips.

3. Divide the mixture among the paper liners and sprinkle with the remaining chocolate chips. Bake in the preheated oven for 15–20 minutes, or until risen, firm, and golden brown. Transfer the cupcakes to a wire rack to cool.

4. When cooled, drizzle the cakes with the melted chocolate and decorate with pieces of chocolate mint sticks. Let set.

**Makes 32**

* 1½ cups all-purpose flour
* 1 tbsp baking powder
* ¾ cup unsalted butter, softened
* generous ¾ cup superfine sugar
* 3 eggs, beaten
* 1 tsp peppermint extract
  scant ½ cup semisweet chocolate chips

**Topping**
3½ oz/100 g semisweet chocolate, melted
10 mint chocolate sticks, broken into short lengths

# 60

# Marzipan Chunk Cupcakes

1. Preheat the oven to 375°F/190°C. Put 32 paper liners into shallow muffin pans or put double-layer liners onto cookie sheets.

2. Sift the flour, cornstarch, and baking powder into a large bowl and add the butter, sugar, eggs, and almond extract. Beat well until the mixture is smooth.

3. Divide the mixture among the paper liners and sprinkle a few pieces of marzipan on top of each. Bake in the preheated oven for 15–20 minutes, or until risen, firm, and golden brown. Transfer the cupcakes to a wire rack to cool.

**Makes 32**

* 1½ cups all-purpose flour
* 2 tsp cornstarch
* 1 tbsp baking powder
* ¾ cup unsalted butter, softened
* generous ¾ cup superfine sugar
* 3 eggs, beaten
* 1 tsp almond extract
* 3 oz/85 g golden marzipan, cut into ¼-inch/5-mm dice

# Fruity

# 61

# Raspberry & Pine Nut Bars

1. Preheat the oven to 350°F/180°C. Grease and line an 8 x 12-inch/20 x 30-cm rectangular cake pan.

2. Sift the flour and baking powder into a large bowl and add the butter, sugar, eggs, and vanilla extract. Beat well until the mixture is smooth, then stir in the milk, raspberries, and half the pine nuts.

3. Spoon the mixture into the prepared pan and smooth the surface with a spatula. Sprinkle the remaining pine nuts over the surface. Bake in the preheated oven for 40–50 minutes, or until risen, firm, and golden brown.

4. Let cool in the pan, then cut into bars when firm.

**Makes 10**

* oil or melted butter, for greasing
* 1½ cups all-purpose flour
* 1 tbsp baking powder
* ¾ cup unsalted butter, softened
* generous ¾ cup superfine sugar
* 3 eggs, beaten
* 1 tsp vanilla extract
* 2 tbsp milk
* 1⅓ cups fresh raspberries
* ⅔ cup pine nuts

# 62

# Rhubarb & Ginger Cake

1. Preheat the oven to 350°F/180°C. Grease and line a 9-inch/23-cm square, deep cake pan.

2. Sift the flour and baking powder into a large bowl and add the butter, superfine sugar, eggs, and vanilla extract. Beat well until the mixture is smooth.

3. Spoon the mixture into the prepared pan and smooth the surface with a spatula. Stir the cornstarch into the rhubarb, then add the ginger and sprinkle evenly over the cake mixture.

4. Bake in the preheated oven for 50–60 minutes, or until risen, firm, and golden brown. Let cool in the pan for about 10 minutes, until firm, then turn out and finish cooling on a wire rack.

5. For the icing, mix the confectioners' sugar with the ginger syrup until smooth, then drizzle it over the cake. Let set before cutting into bars or squares.

**Serves 8**

* oil or melted butter, for greasing
* 1½ cups all-purpose flour
  2 tsp baking powder
* ¾ cup unsalted butter, softened
* generous ¾ cup superfine sugar
* 3 eggs, beaten
* 1 tsp vanilla extract
  1 tbsp cornstarch
  7 oz/200 g pink rhubarb, cut into ½-inch/1-cm slices
  2 tbsp finely chopped preserved ginger

Icing
3 tbsp confectioners' sugar
1 tbsp preserved ginger syrup (from the jar)

# 63

# Pear & Hazelnut Streusel Cake

1. Preheat the oven to 350°F/180°C. Grease and line a 9-inch/23-cm round, springform cake pan.

2. For the streusel topping, combine the chopped hazelnuts, brown sugar, flour, cinnamon, and melted butter in a small bowl with a fork to make a crumbly mixture.

3. Sift the flour and baking powder into a large bowl and add the butter, superfine sugar, eggs, and vanilla extract. Beat well until the mixture is smooth, then stir in the ground hazelnuts and half the pears.

4. Spoon the mixture into the prepared pan and smooth the surface with a spatula. Sprinkle the remaining pears over the top and spread level. Sprinkle the streusel topping evenly over the cake.

5. Bake in the preheated oven for about 1 hour, or until risen and firm. Let cool in the pan for 2–3 minutes, then remove the sides of the pan and finish cooling on a wire rack.

**Serves 8**

* oil or melted butter, for greasing
* 1½ cups all-purpose flour
  2 tsp baking powder
* ¾ cup unsalted butter, softened
* generous ¾ cup superfine sugar
* 3 eggs, beaten
* 1 tsp vanilla extract
  ½ cup ground hazelnuts
  2 firm ripe pears, peeled, cored, and finely chopped

**Streusel topping**
scant ½ cup finely chopped toasted hazelnuts
scant ¼ cup dark brown sugar
3 tbsp all-purpose flour
½ tsp ground cinnamon
2 tbsp unsalted butter, melted

# 64

# Chewy Date & Sesame Bars

1. Preheat the oven to 350°F/180°C. Grease and line a 12 x 9-inch/30 x 23-cm rectangular cake pan.

2. Put the dates and orange juice into a pan and heat until boiling, stirring occasionally. Reduce the heat and simmer gently for about 5 minutes, until the liquid is absorbed. Remove from the heat and let cool.

3. Sift the flours and baking powder in a large bowl, adding any bran left in the sifter. Add the butter, sugar, eggs, and vanilla extract. Beat well until the mixture is smooth, then stir in the soaked dates.

4. Spoon the mixture into the prepared pan and smooth the surface with a spatula. Sprinkle the sesame seeds over the top. Bake in the preheated oven for 25–30 minutes, or until risen, firm, and golden brown.

5. Let cool in the pan and cut into bars when firm.

**Makes 12**

* oil or melted butter, for greasing
generous 1 cup coarsely chopped pitted dried dates
4 tbsp orange juice
¾ cup all-purpose flour
¾ cup whole-wheat flour
1½ tsp baking powder
* ¾ cup unsalted butter, softened
* generous ¾ cup dark brown sugar
* 3 eggs, beaten
* 1 tsp vanilla extract
3 tbsp sesame seeds

# 65

# Honeyed Apple Bars

1. Preheat the oven to 350°F/180°C. Grease and line a 12 x 9-inch/30 x 23-cm rectangular cake pan.

2. Sift the flour, baking powder, and allspice into a large bowl and add the butter, sugar, eggs, and vanilla extract. Beat well until the mixture is smooth, then stir in the apple juice.

3. Spoon the mixture into the prepared pan and smooth the surface with a spatula. Core and slice the apples and arrange them, overlapping, on top of the cake mixture, without pressing into the mix. Brush lightly with half the honey.

4. Bake in the preheated oven for 30–35 minutes, or until risen, firm, and golden brown. Let cool in the pan for about 15 minutes, until firm, then cut into bars and finish cooling on a wire rack.

5. Brush with the remaining honey before serving.

**Makes 12**

* oil or melted butter, for greasing
* 1½ cups all-purpose flour
* 2 tsp baking powder
* ½ tsp ground allspice
* ¾ cup unsalted butter, softened
* generous ¾ cup superfine sugar
* 3 eggs, beaten
* 1 tsp vanilla extract
* 2 tbsp apple juice
* 4 red-skinned apples
* 3 tbsp honey, warmed

# Banana Pecan Cake

1. Preheat the oven to 350°F/180°C. Grease and line the bottoms of two 8-inch/20-cm layer cake pans.

2. Sift the flour and baking powder into a large bowl and add the butter, sugar, eggs, and vanilla extract. Beat well until the mixture is smooth, then stir in the chopped pecans. Add the dulce de leche and stir to swirl through the mix.

3. Spoon the mixture into the prepared pans and smooth the surfaces with a spatula. Bake in the preheated oven for 25–30 minutes, or until risen, firm, and golden brown. Let cool in the pans for 2–3 minutes, then turn out and finish cooling on a wire rack.

4. Reserve a few slices of banana for decoration and mash the remainder. Mix the mashed bananas with 3 tablespoons of the dulce de leche and use to sandwich the cakes together.

5. Whip the cream until thick, then swirl in the remaining dulce de leche. Spread over the cake and decorate with the reserved banana slices and the pecan halves.

**Serves 6**

* oil or melted butter, for greasing
* 1½ cups all-purpose flour
* 1 tbsp baking powder
* ¾ cup unsalted butter, softened
* generous ¾ cup superfine sugar
* 3 eggs, beaten
* 1 tsp vanilla extract
  ⅓ cup finely chopped pecans
  scant ¼ cup dulce de leche

**Filling and topping**
2 bananas
5 tbsp dulce de leche
scant ½ cup heavy cream
pecan halves, to decorate

# Tropical Fruit Ring

1. Preheat the oven to 325°F/160°C. Grease a 6¾-cup tube cake pan, preferably nonstick. Stir the lime juice into the dried tropical fruit and let soak for 15 minutes.

2. Sift the flour and baking powder into a large bowl and add the butter, superfine sugar, eggs, and vanilla extract. Beat well until the mixture is smooth, then stir in the soaked fruit.

3. Spoon the mixture into the prepared pan and level the top with a spatula. Bake in the preheated oven for 40–50 minutes, or until risen, firm, and golden brown. Let cool in the pan for 10 minutes, then turn out and finish cooling on a wire rack.

4. For the icing, sift the confectioners' sugar into a bowl, add the lime juice, and stir until smooth. Spoon the icing over the cake and decorate with dried tropical fruit. Let set before slicing.

**Serves 12**

* oil or melted butter, for greasing
* 2 tbsp lime juice
  scant ½ cup finely chopped dried tropical fruit, such as mango, papaya and/or pineapple, plus extra to decorate
* 1½ cups all-purpose flour
  2½ tsp baking powder
* ¾ cup unsalted butter, softened
* generous ¾ cup superfine sugar
* 3 eggs, beaten
* 1 tsp vanilla extract

Icing
⅔ cup confectioners' sugar
1 tbsp lime juice

# 68

# Berry Crunch Cake

① Preheat the oven to 350°F/180°C. Grease and line the bottom of a 9-inch/23-cm round, springform cake pan.

② Sift the 1½ cups flour and the baking powder into a large bowl and add the butter, sugar, eggs, and vanilla extract. Beat well until the mixture is smooth.

③ Spoon about half the mixture into the prepared pan and smooth the surface with a spatula. Spread the berries evenly over the mixture. Stir the extra tablespoon of flour into the remaining mix. Spread out the crushed cookies on a large plate. Using 2 spoons, toss about 20 small spoonfuls of the mix in the crushed cookies, then arrange over the cake. Sprinkle over any remaining cookie crumbs.

④ Bake in the preheated oven for 45–55 minutes, or until risen, firm, and golden brown. Let cool in the pan for 2–3 minutes, then remove the sides and finish cooling on a wire rack. Best eaten on the day of making.

**Serves 8**

* oil or melted butter, for greasing
* 1½ cups all-purpose flour, plus 1 tbsp
  2 tsp baking powder
* ¾ cup unsalted butter, softened
* generous ¾ cup superfine sugar
* 3 eggs, beaten
* 1 tsp vanilla extract
  2 cups fresh mixed berries, such as raspberries, blueberries, and blackberries
  1¼ cups crushed gingersnaps

# Mango & Ginger Roulade

1. Preheat the oven to 350°F/180°C. Grease and line a 9 x 13-inch/23 x 33-cm jelly roll pan with the paper ½ inch/1 cm above the rim. Lay a sheet of parchment paper on the counter and sprinkle with superfine sugar.

2. Sift the flour and baking powder into a large bowl and add the butter, sugar, eggs, and vanilla extract. Beat well until the mixture is smooth, then beat in the orange juice.

3. Spoon the mixture into the prepared pan and smooth into the corners with a spatula. Bake in the preheated oven for 15–20 minutes, or until risen, firm, and golden brown.

4. Meanwhile, peel and pit the mango. Chop finely and reserve a little for decoration. Transfer the remaining mango to a small bowl and stir in 2 tablespoons of the candied ginger.

5. When baked, carefully turn out the sponge cake onto the sugared parchment paper and spread with the mango mixture. Roll up the sponge cake firmly from one short side to enclose the mango, keeping the paper around the outside to hold it in place. Lift onto a wire rack to cool, removing the paper when firm.

6. When cold, top with spoonfuls of sour cream and decorate with the reserved mango and the remaining candied ginger.

**Serves 6**

- oil or melted butter, for greasing
- 1⅓ cups all-purpose flour
- 1½ tsp baking powder
- ¾ cup unsalted butter, softened
- generous ¾ cup superfine sugar, plus extra for sprinkling
- 3 eggs, beaten
- 1 tsp vanilla extract
- 2 tbsp orange juice
- 1 large ripe mango
- 3 tbsp chopped candied ginger
- 5 tbsp sour cream

# Banana & Carrot Squares

1. Preheat the oven to 325°F/160°C. Grease and line a 9-inch/23-cm square cake pan.

2. Sift the flour, baking powder, and nutmeg into a bowl and add the butter, superfine sugar, and eggs. Beat well until smooth, then stir in the lemon juice, banana, carrots, and walnuts.

3. Spoon the mixture into the pan and spread the top level. Bake in the preheated oven for 45–55 minutes, or until well risen, firm, and golden brown.

4. Let cool in the pan for 5 minutes, then turn out onto a wire rack to finish cooling. Cut into squares when cold.

5. For the frosting, combine the ricotta, confectioners' sugar, and lemon rind in a small bowl. Spoon or pipe a little frosting onto each square of cake, top with a banana chip, and sprinkle with nutmeg.

**Makes 16**

* oil or melted butter, for greasing
* 1½ cups all-purpose flour
* 1 tbsp baking powder
  1 tsp ground nutmeg
* ¾ cup unsalted butter, softened
* generous ¾ cup superfine sugar
* 3 eggs, beaten
  1 tbsp lemon juice
  1 banana, mashed
  1 cup coarsely grated carrots
  ⅓ cup finely chopped walnuts
  dried banana chips and freshly grated nutmeg, to decorate

**Frosting**
generous 1 cup ricotta cheese
⅔ cup confectioners' sugar
finely grated rind of ½ lemon

# 71

# Peachy Oat Crumble Cake

1. Preheat the oven to 350°F/180°C. Grease and line the bottom of a 10-inch/25-cm round, springform cake pan.

2. Sift the flour, baking powder, and star anise into a large bowl and add the butter, sugar, eggs, and vanilla extract. Beat well until the mixture is smooth.

3. Spoon the mixture into the prepared pan and smooth the surface with a spatula. Arrange the chopped peaches evenly over the mixture.

4. For the topping, combine the oats and sugar in a small bowl. Melt the butter, then stir into the bowl to make a crumbly mix. Spread evenly over the peaches.

5. Bake in the preheated oven for about 1 hour, or until risen, firm, and golden brown. Let cool in the pan for 2–3 minutes, then remove the sides and finish cooling on a wire rack. Best eaten on the day of making.

**Serves 8–10**

* oil or melted butter, for greasing
* 1½ cups all-purpose flour
* 1 tbsp baking powder
  1 tsp ground star anise
* ¾ cup unsalted butter, softened
* generous ¾ cup superfine sugar
* 3 eggs, beaten
* 1 tsp vanilla extract
  4 ripe peaches, pitted and coarsely chopped

**Topping**
1¼ cups rolled oats

generous ¼ cup superfine sugar

4 tbsp unsalted butter

# Chunky Orange & Peanut Squares

1. Preheat the oven to 325°F/160°C. Grease and line a 9-inch/23-cm square cake pan.

2. Finely grate the rind from the orange and reserve. Use a sharp knife to cut off all the peel and white pith, then cut the flesh into small chunks.

3. Sift the flour and baking powder into a large bowl and add the butter, peanut butter, superfine sugar, eggs, and vanilla extract. Beat well until the mixture is smooth, then stir in the reserved orange rind and orange chunks.

4. Spoon the mixture into the prepared pan and smooth the surface with a spatula. Bake in the preheated oven for 40–50 minutes, or until risen, firm, and golden brown. Let cool in the pan for about 10 minutes, then turn out and finish cooling on a wire rack.

5. For the frosting, combine the peanut butter, orange juice, and confectioners' sugar evenly, then spread over the cooled cake. Cut into squares before serving.

**Makes 9**

* oil or melted butter, for greasing
1 orange
* 1½ cups all-purpose flour
1½ tsp baking powder
scant ½ cup unsalted butter, softened
⅓ cup crunchy peanut butter
* generous ¾ cup superfine sugar
* 3 eggs, beaten
* 1 tsp vanilla extract

**Frosting**
¼ cup crunchy peanut butter
2 tbsp orange juice
½ cup confectioners' sugar

# Seeded Pear Bars

1. Preheat the oven to 350°F/180°C. Grease and line a 12 x 9-inch/30 x 23-cm rectangular cake pan.

2. Cut the pears into quarters, remove the cores, and cut each quarter into 3–4 long slices. Brush with half the lemon juice.

3. Sift the flour and baking powder into a large bowl and add the butter, light brown sugar, eggs, and vanilla extract. Beat well until the mixture is smooth. Stir in the remaining lemon juice, the lemon rind, oats, and sunflower and pumpkin seeds.

4. Spoon the mixture into the prepared pan and smooth the surface with a spatula. Arrange the pear slices overlapping on top, without pressing into the mix, and sprinkle with the raw brown sugar.

5. Bake in the preheated oven for 35–40 minutes, or until risen, firm, and golden brown. Let cool in the pan for about 15 minutes, until firm, then cut into bars and finish cooling on a wire rack.

**Makes 14**

- oil or melted butter, for greasing
- 3 firm ripe pears
- 2 tbsp lemon juice
- 1½ cups all-purpose flour
- 2 tsp baking powder
- ¾ cup unsalted butter, softened
- generous ¾ cup light brown sugar
- 3 eggs, beaten
- 1 tsp vanilla extract
- finely grated rind of 1 lemon
- ½ cup rolled oats
- 3 tbsp sunflower seeds
- ¼ cup pumpkin seeds
- 1 tbsp raw brown sugar

# 74

# Strawberry Sponge Layer Cake

1. Preheat the oven to 350°F/180°C. Grease and line a 9 x 13-inch/23 x 33-cm jelly roll pan with the paper ½ inch/ 1 cm above the rim.

2. Sift the flour and baking powder into a large bowl and add the butter, superfine sugar, eggs, and vanilla extract. Beat well until the mixture is smooth, then beat in the milk.

3. Spoon the mixture into the prepared pan and smooth into the corners with a spatula. Bake in the preheated oven for 15–20 minutes, or until risen, firm, and golden brown. Let cool in the pan.

4. When the cake is cold, cut crosswise into three rectangles. Hull and chop the strawberries, reserving 4–5 for decoration. Stir the chopped strawberries into the mascarpone and use to sandwich together the cakes.

5. To serve, dust the cake with confectioners' sugar. Hull and slice the reserved strawberries and arrange on top.

**Serves 6–8**

* oil or melted butter, for greasing

1⅓ cups all-purpose flour

1½ tsp baking powder

* ¾ cup unsalted butter, softened

* generous ¾ cup superfine sugar

* 3 eggs, beaten

* 1 tsp vanilla extract

* 2 tbsp milk

scant 2 cups fresh strawberries

generous 1 cup mascarpone cheese

confectioners' sugar, for dusting

# Blueberry Orange Streusel Cake

1. Preheat the oven to 325°F/160°C. Grease and line the bottom of a 9-inch/23-cm round, springform cake pan.

2. For the topping, put all the ingredients into a bowl and mix with a fork to make a crumbly mixture.

3. Sift the flour and baking powder into a large bowl and add the butter, sugar, eggs, and vanilla extract. Beat well until the mixture is smooth, then add the orange rind, ground almonds, and half the blueberries.

4. Spoon the mixture into the prepared pan, smooth level with a spatula, and sprinkle with the remaining blueberries. Spread the crumble topping evenly over the top, covering completely.

5. Bake in the preheated oven for 1 hour–1 hour 10 minutes, or until risen, firm, and golden brown. Let cool in the pan for 10 minutes, then remove the sides of the pan and finish cooling on a wire rack.

**Serves 8–10**

* oil or melted butter, for greasing
* 1½ cups all-purpose flour
  2 tsp baking powder
* ¾ cup unsalted butter, softened
* generous ¾ cup superfine sugar
* 3 eggs, beaten
* 1 tsp vanilla extract
  finely grated rind of ½ orange
  ½ cup ground almonds
  generous 1 cup fresh blueberries

Topping
½ cup all-purpose flour
2 tbsp unsalted butter, softened
2 tbsp superfine sugar
finely grated rind of ½ orange

# Kiwi Cake with Lemon Frosting

1. Preheat the oven to 325°F/160°C. Grease and line a 5-cup loaf pan.

2. Sift the flour and baking powder into a large bowl and add the butter, superfine sugar, eggs, and vanilla extract. Beat well until the mixture is smooth. Stir in half the chopped kiwi.

3. Spoon the mixture into the prepared pan and smooth the surface with a spatula. Sprinkle with the remaining chopped kiwi. Bake in the preheated oven for about 1 hour, or until risen, firm, and golden brown.

4. Let cool in the pan for 10 minutes, then turn out and finish cooling on a wire rack.

5. For the frosting, beat together the cream cheese, lemon rind, and confectioners' sugar until smooth. Spread the frosting over the cake and top with kiwi slices.

**Serves 8**

* oil or melted butter, for greasing
* 1½ cups all-purpose flour
  2 tsp baking powder
* ¾ cup unsalted butter, softened
* generous ¾ cup superfine sugar
* 3 eggs, beaten
* 1 tsp vanilla extract
  2 kiwis, peeled and chopped into ½-inch/1-cm dice
  kiwi slices, to decorate

Frosting
¼ cup cream cheese
1 tbsp grated lemon rind
1 cup confectioners' sugar

# 77

# Chunky Apricot Loaf

1. Preheat the oven to 325°F/160°C. Grease and line a 5-cup loaf pan.

2. Sift the flour and baking powder into a large bowl and add the butter, sugar, eggs, and almond extract. Beat well until the mixture is smooth, then stir in the orange juice and ⅔ cup of the apricots.

3. Spoon the mixture into the prepared pan and smooth the surface with a spatula. Sprinkle with the remaining apricots. Bake in the preheated oven for about 1 hour, or until risen, firm, and golden brown.

4. Let cool in the pan for 10 minutes, then turn out and finish cooling on a wire rack.

5. Warm the apricot jelly in a pan with the lemon juice and brush lightly over the top of the cake. Cut into slices to serve.

**Serves 8**

* oil or melted butter, for greasing
* 2¼ cups all-purpose flour
* 2 tsp baking powder
* ¾ cup unsalted butter, softened
* generous ¾ cup superfine sugar
* 3 eggs, beaten
* 1 tsp almond extract
* 2 tbsp orange juice
* scant 1 cup chopped plumped dried apricots
* 3 tbsp apricot jelly
* 1 tbsp lemon juice

# Cranberry Coconut Ring

1. Preheat the oven to 350°F/180°C. Grease a 6¾-cup tube cake pan, preferably nonstick.

2. Sift the flour and baking powder into a large bowl and add the butter, sugar, eggs, and vanilla extract. Beat well until the mixture is smooth. Stir in the cranberries, cranberry juice, and dry unsweetened coconut.

3. Spoon the mixture into the prepared pan and smooth the surface with a spatula. Bake in the preheated oven for 30–35 minutes, or until risen, firm, and golden brown.

4. Let cool in the pan for 5 minutes, then turn out and finish cooling on a wire rack. Spoon the cranberry sauce on top of the cake, then sprinkle with coconut shreds and serve.

**Serves 10**

* oil or melted butter, for greasing
* 1½ cups all-purpose flour
* 1 tbsp baking powder
* ¾ cup unsalted butter, softened
* generous ¾ cup superfine sugar
* 3 eggs, beaten
* 1 tsp vanilla extract
  ½ cup dried cranberries
* 2 tbsp cranberry juice
  ⅔ cup dry unsweetened coconut
  3 tbsp cranberry sauce
  2 tbsp toasted long-shred coconut

# Pineapple Hummingbird Cake

1. Preheat the oven to 350°F/180°C. Grease and line the bottoms of three 9-inch/23-cm layer cake pans.

2. Sift the flour, baking powder, and cinnamon into a bowl and add the superfine sugar, oil, eggs, and vanilla extract. Beat well until the mixture is smooth, then stir in the pecans, banana, and crushed pineapple.

3. Divide the mixture among the prepared pans, spreading it evenly. Bake in the preheated oven for 20-25 minutes, or until risen, firm, and golden brown.

4. Let cool in the pans for 2–3 minutes, then turn out onto wire racks to finish cooling.

5. For the frosting, beat together the cream cheese, butter, vanilla extract, and confectioners' sugar until smooth. Sandwich the cakes together with about two-thirds of the frosting. Spread the remaining frosting on top, then decorate with pineapple pieces and pecan halves.

**Serves 8–10**

* oil or melted butter, for greasing
* 1½ cups all-purpose flour
* 1 tbsp baking powder
* 1 tsp ground cinnamon
* generous ¾ cup superfine sugar
* ¾ cup sunflower oil
* 3 eggs, beaten
* 1 tsp vanilla extract
* ½ cup finely chopped pecans
* 2 small ripe bananas, mashed
* ⅓ cup crushed pineapple
* pineapple pieces and pecan halves, to decorate

Frosting
¾ cup whole-fat cream cheese
¼ cup unsalted butter, softened
1 tsp vanilla extract
3½ cups confectioners' sugar, sifted

# 80

# Chocolate & Cherry Gâteau

1  Preheat the oven to 350°F/180°C. Grease and line the bottoms of two 8-inch/20-cm layer cake pans.

2  Sift the flour, cocoa, and baking powder into a large bowl and add the butter, superfine sugar, eggs, and vanilla extract. Beat well until the mixture is smooth and stir in the milk.

3  Divide the mixture between the prepared pans and smooth the tops with a spatula. Bake in the preheated oven for 25–30 minutes, or until risen and firm to the touch. Let cool in the pans for 2–3 minutes, then turn out and finish cooling on wire racks.

4  When the cakes are cold, sprinkle with the Kirsch, if using. Whip the cream with the confectioners' sugar until thick, then spread about a third over the top of one of the cakes. Spread the cherries over the cream mixture and place the second cake on top.

5  Spread the remaining cream mixture over the top and sides of the cake and decorate with grated chocolate and fresh whole cherries.

**Serves 8**

* oil or melted butter, for greasing
  1⅓ cups all-purpose flour
  2 tbsp unsweetened cocoa
* 1 tbsp baking powder
* ¾ cup unsalted butter, softened
* generous ¾ cup superfine sugar
* 3 eggs, beaten
* 1 tsp vanilla extract
* 2 tbsp milk
  3 tbsp Kirsch or brandy (optional)
  grated chocolate and fresh whole cherries, to decorate

**Filling and topping**
2 cups heavy cream
2 tbsp confectioners' sugar
1⅓ cups fresh or frozen pitted black cherries

# Warming

# 81

# Plum Sponge Cake

1. Preheat the oven to 325°F/160°C. Grease and line a 13 x 9-inch/32 x 23-cm rectangular cake pan.

2. Sift the flour and baking powder into a large bowl and add the butter, superfine sugar, eggs, and almond extract. Beat well until the mixture is smooth, then stir in the ground almonds.

3. Spoon the mixture into the prepared pan and smooth the surface with a spatula. Arrange the plum quarters, skin-side down, over the mixture, without pressing them down, then sprinkle with the slivered almonds and raw brown sugar.

4. Bake in the preheated oven for 50–60 minutes, or until risen and golden brown. Cut into squares and serve warm with cream or yogurt.

**Serves 6**

* oil or melted butter, for greasing
* 1½ cups all-purpose flour
  2 tsp baking powder
* ¾ cup unsalted butter, softened
* generous ¾ cup superfine sugar
* 3 eggs, beaten
* 1 tsp almond extract
  ⅔ cup ground almonds
  8–10 large red plums, pitted and quartered
  3 tbsp slivered almonds
  2 tbsp raw brown sugar
  cream or yogurt, to serve

# 82

# Mango & Coconut Brûlée Cake

1. Preheat the oven to 350°F/180°C. Grease and line the bottom of a 9-inch/23-cm round, deep cake pan.

2. Arrange the mango evenly over the bottom of the pan. Sift the flour and baking powder into a large bowl and add the butter, superfine sugar, and eggs. Beat well until the mixture is smooth, then stir in the lime juice, lime rind, and dry unsweetened coconut.

3. Spoon the mixture over the mango and smooth the surface with a spatula. Bake in the preheated oven for 40–50 minutes, or until risen and golden brown.

4. Let cool in the pan for 2–3 minutes, then turn out onto a flameproof dish. Preheat the broiler to high. Sprinkle the top of the cake with the granulated sugar and place under the hot broiler for 2–3 minutes, until browned. Alternatively, use a chef's blowtorch to brown the top.

5. Serve hot, sprinkled with coconut shreds and cut into slices.

**Serves 6**

* oil or melted butter, for greasing
* 1 large ripe mango, peeled, pitted, and diced
* 1½ cups all-purpose flour
* 1 tbsp baking powder
* ¾ cup unsalted butter, softened
* generous ¾ cup superfine sugar
* 3 eggs, beaten
* 2 tbsp lime juice
* finely grated rind of 1 lime
* ⅓ cup dry unsweetened coconut
* 2 tbsp granulated sugar
* toasted long-shred coconut, to decorate

# Caramel Apple Upside-Down Cake

1. Preheat the oven to 350°F/180°C. Grease a 9-inch/23-cm round, deep cake pan with a solid bottom.

2. For the caramel apple topping, put the butter and sugar into a heavy pan with the water and heat gently until melted, then bring to a boil. Reduce the heat and cook, stirring, until it turns to a deep golden caramel color. Pour quickly into the cake pan, tilting to cover the bottom evenly.

3. Peel, core, and thickly slice the apples, toss in the lemon juice, and spread evenly over the bottom of the cake pan.

4. Sift the flour and baking powder into a large bowl and add the butter, sugar, eggs, and vanilla extract. Beat well until the mixture is smooth, then stir in the lemon rind.

5. Spoon the mixture over the apples and smooth the surface with a spatula. Bake in the preheated oven for 40–50 minutes, or until risen and golden brown.

6. Let cool in the pan for 2–3 minutes, then turn out carefully onto a warmed serving plate. Serve with cream.

## Serves 6

* oil or melted butter, for greasing
* 1½ cups all-purpose flour
* 1 tbsp baking powder
* ¾ cup unsalted butter, softened
* generous ¾ cup superfine sugar
* 3 eggs, beaten
* 1 tsp vanilla extract
* finely grated rind of 1 lemon
* cream, to serve

### Caramel apple topping
¼ cup unsalted butter
½ cup superfine sugar
1 tbsp water
4 apples
2 tbsp lemon juice

# 84

# Mocha Desserts

1. Preheat the oven to 400°F/200°C. Grease and line six 1-cup individual metal bowls.

2. Sift the flour, cocoa, and baking powder into a large bowl and add the butter, sugar, eggs, and coffee extract. Beat well until the mixture is smooth.

3. Spoon the mixture into the prepared bowls and smooth the surfaces with a spatula. Place a square of chocolate on top of each. Bake in the preheated oven for 20–25 minutes, or until risen and firm to the touch.

4. For the sauce, put the cream, chocolate, and coffee extract into a small pan and heat gently without boiling, stirring, until melted and smooth. Turn out the desserts and serve with the sauce poured over them.

## Makes 6

* oil or melted butter, for greasing
* 1½ cups all-purpose flour
* 2 tbsp unsweetened cocoa
* 2 tsp baking powder
* ¾ cup unsalted butter, softened
* generous ¾ cup light brown sugar
* 3 eggs, beaten
* 1 tsp coffee extract
* 6 small squares semisweet chocolate

### Sauce
generous 1 cup light cream

3½ oz/100 g semisweet chocolate, broken into pieces

1 tsp coffee extract

# 85

# Lemon Surprise Cakes

1. Preheat the oven to 350°F/180°C. Grease six 1-cup ovenproof teacups or ramekins and place in a roasting pan.

2. Sift the flour and baking powder into a large bowl and add the butter, sugar, and egg yolks. Beat well until the mixture is smooth, then stir in the lemon rind, lemon juice, and milk. In a separate bowl, whisk the egg whites until they hold stiff peaks. Fold into the creamed mixture.

3. Spoon the mixture into the prepared teacups. Pour hot water into the pan to come halfway up the sides of the cups. Bake in the preheated oven for 30–35 minutes, or until risen, firm, and golden brown.

4. Transfer the teacups to warmed serving plates. There should be a light "custard" layer under the surface.

## Makes 6

* oil or melted butter, for greasing
* 1½ cups all-purpose flour
* 1 tbsp baking powder
* ¾ cup unsalted butter, softened
* generous ¾ cup superfine sugar
* 3 eggs, separated
  finely grated rind and juice of 2 lemons
  ⅔ cup milk

# Peach & Cinnamon Pie

1. Preheat the oven to 325°F/160°C. Grease and line the bottom of a 9-inch/23-cm round, springform cake pan.

2. Sift the flour, baking powder, and cinnamon into a large bowl and add the butter, sugar, eggs, and vanilla extract. Beat well until the mixture is smooth.

3. Spoon half the mixture into the prepared pan and smooth the surface with a spatula. Arrange the peaches on top. Stir the cornflakes lightly into the remaining mixture and drop spoonfuls of the mix over the peaches.

4. Bake in the preheated oven for about 1 hour, or until risen, firm, and golden brown. Serve hot with cream.

**Serves 6**

* oil or melted butter, for greasing
* 1½ cups all-purpose flour
  2 tsp baking powder
  1 tsp ground cinnamon
* ¾ cup unsalted butter, softened
* ¾ cup superfine sugar
* 3 eggs, beaten
* 1 tsp vanilla extract
  3 ripe peaches or nectarines, peeled, pitted, and coarsely chopped
  2½ cups corn flakes, lightly crushed
  cream, to serve

# Whole Orange & Almond Cake

1. Preheat the oven to 325°F/160°C. Grease and line a 9-inch/23-cm round, deep cake pan.

2. Wash the oranges and put into a pan, then cover with boiling water and simmer, covered, for 1 hour, until soft. Drain and let cool slightly, then cut in half and remove any seeds. Process in a food processor or blender until smooth, then stir in the ground almonds.

3. Sift the flour and baking powder into a large bowl and add the butter, sugar, eggs, and orange flower water. Beat well until the mixture is smooth. Add the orange-and-almond mixture and the orange juice, mixing evenly.

4. Spoon the mixture into the prepared pan and smooth the surface with a spatula. Bake in the preheated oven for 40–50 minutes, or until firm and golden brown.

5. Let cool in the pan for 2–3 minutes, then turn out and serve warm, topped with slivered almonds and strips of orange zest.

**Serves 8–10**

* oil or melted butter, for greasing
* 2 oranges
* ½ cup ground almonds
* 1 cup all-purpose flour
* 1 tbsp baking powder
* 6 tbsp unsalted butter, softened
* generous ¾ cup superfine sugar
* 3 eggs, beaten
* 1 tsp orange flower water
* 2 tbsp orange juice
* 2 tbsp toasted slivered almonds
* strips of orange zest, to decorate

# 88

# Lime Halva Cake

1. Preheat the oven to 350°F/180°C. Grease and line an 8-inch/20-cm square, deep cake pan.

2. Sift the semolina and baking powder into a large bowl and add the butter, sugar, and eggs. Beat well until the mixture is smooth. Stir in the ground almonds and lime rind and juice.

3. Spoon the mixture into the prepared pan and smooth the surface with a spatula. Bake in the preheated oven for 30–35 minutes, or until risen and golden brown.

4. Meanwhile, to make the syrup, put the lime juice, sugar, water, and cinnamon stick into a pan and heat gently, stirring, until the sugar dissolves. Add the lime slices and simmer for 1–2 minutes, then remove them carefully and set aside. Bring the syrup to a boil and boil for 6–8 minutes, until syrupy and reduced by half. Discard the cinnamon stick.

5. Turn out the cake and arrange the lime slices over the top. Spoon the lime syrup evenly over it and serve warm.

**Serves 9**

* oil or melted butter, for greasing

1½ cups semolina

* 1 tbsp baking powder

* ¾ cup unsalted butter, softened

* generous ¾ cup superfine sugar

* 3 eggs, beaten

scant 1 cup ground almonds

finely grated rind and juice of 1 lime

**Syrup**
juice of 2 limes

generous ¾ cup superfine sugar

scant 1 cup water

1 cinnamon stick

1 lime, thinly sliced

# Apple Cider Cake

1. Preheat the oven to 325°F/160°C. Grease an 8¾-cup rectangular ovenproof dish, about 2¼ inches/5.5 cm deep.

2. Cut a fairly thick slice from the stalk end of the apples and reserve. Remove the core from the apples, then replace the tops.

3. Sift the flour and baking powder into a large bowl and add the butter, superfine sugar, eggs, and vanilla extract. Beat well until the mixture is smooth, then beat in the hard cider.

4. Spoon the mixture into the prepared dish and smooth the surface with a spatula. Press the apples into the mixture, then brush with butter. Combine the cinnamon and raw brown sugar and sprinkle it over the apples.

5. Bake in the preheated oven for 1–1¼ hours, or until risen, firm, and golden brown. Serve warm, with cream or yogurt.

**Serves 6**

* melted butter, for greasing and brushing
  6 small apples
* 1½ cups all-purpose flour
  2 tsp baking powder
* ¾ cup unsalted butter, softened
* generous ¾ cup superfine sugar
* 3 eggs, beaten
* 1 tsp vanilla extract
* 2 tbsp hard cider
  ¼ tsp ground cinnamon
  1 tbsp raw brown sugar
  cream or yogurt, to serve

# Apple & Blackberry Sponge Cake

1. Preheat the oven to 325°F/160°C. Grease a 6¾-cup ovenproof bowl.

2. Peel and core the apple and cut half into dice, then mix with the blackberries and raw brown sugar. Spoon into the bottom of the prepared bowl. Coarsely grate the remaining apple.

3. Sift the flour and baking powder into a bowl and add the butter, superfine sugar, eggs, and vanilla extract. Beat well until smooth, then stir in the grated apple.

4. Spoon the mixture into the bowl and spread the top level. Bake for 1 hour–1 hour 10 minutes, or until well risen, firm, and golden brown.

5. Let cool in the bowl for 2 minutes, then turn out onto a warmed serving plate. Serve with cream.

**Serves 6–8**

* oil or melted butter, for greasing
* 1 baking apple
* ⅔ cup fresh blackberries
* 2 tbsp raw brown sugar
* 1½ cups all-purpose flour
* 2 tsp baking powder
* ¾ cup unsalted butter, softened
* generous ¾ cup superfine sugar
* 3 eggs, beaten
* 1 tsp vanilla extract
* cream, to serve

# Individual Golden Raisin Syrup Sponge Cakes

1. Preheat the oven to 325°F/160°C. Grease a 12-cup muffin pan and place a teaspoonful of the corn syrup in each cup.

2. Sift the flours, baking powder, and allspice into a large bowl, adding any bran left in the sifter. Add the butter, sugar, eggs, and vanilla extract. Beat well until the mixture is smooth, then stir in half the golden raisins.

3. Divide the mixture among the prepared cups in the muffin pan and sprinkle the remaining golden raisins on top. Bake in the preheated oven for 20–25 minutes, or until risen, firm, and golden brown.

4. Let stand for 2 minutes, then turn out onto warmed serving plates. Serve with cream.

**Makes 12**

* oil or melted butter, for greasing

4 tbsp dark corn syrup

generous 1 cup all-purpose flour

½ cup whole-wheat flour

* 1 tbsp baking powder

1 tsp ground allspice

* ¾ cup unsalted butter, softened

* generous ¾ cup superfine sugar

* 3 eggs, beaten

* 1 tsp vanilla extract

scant ½ cup golden raisins

cream, to serve

# Cherry Puff Dessert

1. Preheat the oven to 350°F/180°C. Grease an 8¾-cup ovenproof dish, about 2¼ inches/5.5 cm deep.

2. Sift the 1½ cups flour with the baking powder into a bowl and add the butter, superfine sugar, eggs, and almond extract. Beat well until the mixture is smooth. Stir the 2 tablespoons flour into the cherries, then stir half the cherries into the mix.

3. In a separate bowl, whisk the egg whites until they hold soft peaks. Fold into the creamed mixture using a large metal spoon.

4. Spoon the mixture into the prepared dish and sprinkle with the remaining cherries. Bake in the preheated oven for 45–55 minutes, or until well risen and golden brown.

5. Sprinkle the slivered almonds over the dessert, then dust with confectioners' sugar and serve immediately.

**Serves 6–8**

* oil or melted butter, for greasing
* 1½ cups all-purpose flour, plus 2 tbsp extra
* 1 tbsp baking powder
* ¾ cup unsalted butter, softened
* generous ¾ cup superfine sugar
* 3 eggs, beaten
* 1 tsp almond extract
  1¾ cups pitted cherries
  2 egg whites
  1 tbsp toasted slivered almonds
  confectioners' sugar, for dusting

# Syrup Apricot Ring

1. Preheat the oven to 350°F/180°C. Brush a 9-inch/23-cm tube cake pan or Bundt pan generously with melted butter.

2. Spoon the syrup over the bottom of the cake pan, tilting to cover evenly. Arrange about 20 apricots in the syrup to cover the bottom of the pan. Finely chop the remaining apricots and put into a small pan with the orange juice. Bring to a boil, then remove from the heat and let stand to absorb the liquid.

3. Sift the flour and baking powder into a large bowl and add the butter, sugar, eggs, and vanilla extract. Beat well until the mixture is smooth, then stir in the lemon rind and the soaked apricots.

4. Spoon the mixture into the pan and smooth the surface with a spatula. Bake in the preheated oven for 35–40 minutes, or until risen and golden brown.

5. Let cool in the pan for 2–3 minutes, then turn out carefully onto a warmed serving plate. Serve with a little extra syrup for drizzling over the top.

**Serves 8**

* melted butter, for greasing
  3 tbsp dark corn syrup, plus extra to serve
  ¾ cup plumped dried apricots
* 2 tbsp orange juice
* 1½ cups all-purpose flour
  2 tsp baking powder
* ¾ cup unsalted butter, softened
* generous ¾ cup light brown sugar
* 3 eggs, beaten
* 1 tsp vanilla extract
  finely grated rind of 1 lemon

# 94

# Gooey Orange Chocolate Chip Cake

1. Preheat the oven to 350°F/180°C. Grease and line a 9-inch/23-cm square cake pan.

2. Finely grate the rind from 1 orange and reserve. Use a sharp knife to cut off all the peel and white pith from both oranges and carefully remove the segments. Chop half the segments into small pieces.

3. Sift the flour and baking powder into a large bowl and add the butter, sugar, eggs, and vanilla extract. Beat well until the mixture is smooth, then stir in the reserved orange rind and chopped orange.

4. Spoon the mixture into the prepared pan and smooth the surface with a spatula. Sprinkle the chocolate chips over the top, spreading to the edges. Bake in the preheated oven for 35–40 minutes, or until risen, firm, and golden brown.

5. For the sauce, put the chocolate, butter, and orange juice into a pan and heat gently, stirring, until melted and smooth. Serve the cake warm, topped with the reserved orange segments and with the sauce spooned over the top.

**Serves 6**

- oil or melted butter, for greasing
- 2 oranges
- 1½ cups all-purpose flour
- 2 tsp baking powder
- ¾ cup unsalted butter, softened
- generous ¾ cup superfine sugar
- 3 eggs, beaten
- 1 tsp vanilla extract
- generous ½ cup semisweet chocolate chips

**Sauce**

- 3 oz/85 g semisweet chocolate
- 3 tbsp unsalted butter
- 3 tbsp orange juice

# Prune & Armagnac Cake

1. Preheat the oven to 325°F/160°C. Grease and line a 9-inch/23-cm round cake pan.

2. Put the prunes into a pan with the apple juice and bring to a boil. Reduce the heat and simmer gently for 10 minutes, until the liquid is absorbed. Spoon the armagnac over them and let cool completely.

3. Sift the flour and baking powder into a large bowl and add the butter, light brown sugar, eggs, and vanilla extract. Beat well until the mixture is smooth.

4. Spoon the mixture into the prepared pan and smooth the surface with a spatula. Drain the prunes well, reserving the juices, and arrange the prunes over the mixture in a single layer.

5. Bake in the preheated oven for 40–50 minutes, or until risen, firm, and golden brown.

6. Turn out onto a warmed serving plate and spoon the reserved juices over the cake. Sprinkle with the raw brown sugar and serve in slices, with cream or yogurt.

**Serves 8**

* oil or melted butter, for greasing
  1⅓ cups plumped dried prunes
  ⅔ cup apple juice
  3 tbsp armagnac or port
* 1½ cups all-purpose flour
  2 tsp baking powder
* ¾ cup unsalted butter, softened
* generous ¾ cup light brown sugar
* 3 eggs, beaten
* 1 tsp vanilla extract
  1 tbsp raw brown sugar
  cream or yogurt, to serve

# Rich Walnut Squares

1. Preheat the oven to 325°F/160°C. Grease and line a 9-inch/23-cm square cake pan.

2. Sift the flour and baking powder into a large bowl and add the butter, sugar, eggs, and coffee extract. Beat well until the mixture is smooth, then stir in the sour cream and chopped walnuts.

3. Spoon the mixture into the prepared pan and smooth the surface with a spatula. Bake in the preheated oven for 40–50 minutes, or until risen and firm to the touch.

4. Let cool in the pan for 2–3 minutes, then turn out onto a warmed serving plate and cut into squares. Put the sour cream and maple syrup into a small pan and heat gently, stirring until melted and smooth.

5. Top each square of cake with a walnut half, spoon over the warm sauce, and serve immediately.

**Makes 9**

* oil or melted butter, for greasing
* 1½ cups all-purpose flour
* 1 tbsp baking powder
* ¾ cup unsalted butter, softened
* generous ¾ cup light brown sugar
* 3 eggs, beaten
* 1 tsp coffee extract
  2 tbsp sour cream
  ½ cup finely chopped walnuts
  walnut halves, to decorate

**Sauce**
4 tbsp sour cream
3 tbsp maple syrup

# 97

# Hot Espresso Cakes

1. Preheat the oven to 350°F/180°C. Grease and line a 7 x 11-inch/18 x 28-cm rectangular cake pan.

2. Sift the flour, baking powder, and cocoa into a large bowl and add the butter, brown sugar, eggs, and vanilla extract. Beat well until the mixture is smooth, then beat in the coffee.

3. Spoon the mixture into the prepared pan and smooth the surface with a spatula. Bake in the preheated oven for 30–35 minutes, or until risen and firm to the touch.

4. Meanwhile, make the sauce. Mix the cornstarch with 2 tablespoons of the coffee, then add to a pan with the remaining coffee, the cream, and brown sugar. Heat gently, stirring, until boiling, then reduce the heat and stir for 2 minutes, or until slightly thickened.

5. Using a 3½-inch/9-cm plain cookie cutter, stamp out 6 circles from the cake (the leftovers can be eaten cold). Place on warmed serving plates and sprinkle each with a few coffee sugar crystals. Spoon over the sauce and serve.

## Makes 6

* oil or melted butter, for greasing
* 1½ cups all-purpose flour
* 1 tbsp baking powder
  1 tbsp unsweetened cocoa
* ¾ cup unsalted butter, softened
* generous ¾ cup light brown sugar
* 3 eggs, beaten
* 1 tsp vanilla extract
  3 tbsp strong espresso coffee, cooled
  coffee sugar crystals, to serve

### Sauce
1 tbsp cornstarch

scant 1 cup strong espresso coffee

scant ½ cup light cream

3 tbsp light brown sugar

# Warm White Chocolate Macadamia Ring

① Preheat the oven to 350°F/180°C. Grease a 6¾-cup tube cake pan, preferably nonstick.

② Put the white chocolate, milk, and vanilla extract into a small pan and heat gently, stirring occasionally, until just melted and smooth. Remove from the heat.

③ Sift the flour and baking powder into a large bowl and add the butter, sugar, and eggs. Beat well until the mixture is smooth, then beat in the melted chocolate mixture. Stir in the chopped nuts, mixing evenly.

④ Spoon the mixture into the prepared pan and smooth the surface with a spatula. Bake in the preheated oven for 35–40 minutes, or until risen, firm, and golden brown.

⑤ Meanwhile, make the sauce. Put the chocolate, cream, and vanilla extract into a pan and heat gently until melted and smooth. Keep warm.

⑥ Let the cake cool in the pan for 2–3 minutes, then turn out carefully onto a warmed serving plate. Drizzle the warm sauce over the cake and sprinkle with nuts, then serve in thick slices.

**Serves 8**

* oil or melted butter, for greasing
  2½ oz/70 g white chocolate
* 2 tbsp milk
* 1 tsp vanilla extract
* 1½ cups all-purpose flour
* 1 tbsp baking powder
* ¾ cup unsalted butter, softened
* generous ¾ cup superfine sugar
* 3 eggs, beaten
  ½ cup finely chopped macadamia nuts, plus extra to decorate

**Sauce**
3½ oz/100 g white chocolate
½ cup light cream
½ tsp vanilla extract

# Currant Bars with Spiced Apple Syrup

1. Put the currants, cinnamon stick, and apple juice into a pan and bring to a boil. Remove from the heat and let stand for several hours or overnight. Drain thoroughly, pressing the juices through a strainer, reserving the juices and cinnamon stick. Set aside the currants.

2. Preheat the oven to 350°F/180°C. Grease and line a 12 x 9-inch/30 x 23-cm rectangular cake pan.

3. Sift the flour and baking powder into a large bowl and add the butter, sugar, eggs, and vanilla extract. Beat well until the mixture is smooth.

4. Stir half the currants into the cake mixture and spoon into the prepared pan. Spread the remaining currants over the cake. Bake in the prepared oven for 30–35 minutes, or until risen, firm, and golden brown.

5. Meanwhile, boil the reserved juices and cinnamon stick rapidly to reduce by about half, until slightly syrupy. Discard the cinnamon stick.

6. Cut the cake into bars and serve warm, with the hot syrup spooned over.

**Makes 8**

¾ cup currants

1 cinnamon stick

1¼ cups apple juice

✳ oil or melted butter, for greasing

✳ 1½ cups all-purpose flour

2 tsp baking powder

✳ ¾ cup unsalted butter, softened

✳ generous ¾ cup superfine sugar

✳ 3 eggs, beaten

✳ 1 tsp vanilla extract

# Greek Yogurt & Honey Cake

1. Preheat the oven to 325°F/160°C. Grease and line the bottom of a 9-inch/23-cm round cake pan.

2. Sift the flour and baking powder into a large bowl and add the yogurt, honey, sugar, eggs, and vanilla extract. Beat well until the mixture is smooth.

3. Pour the mixture into the prepared pan. Bake in the preheated oven for 45–55 minutes, or until risen, firm, and golden brown.

4. Let cool in the pan for 2–3 minutes, then turn out onto a serving plate.

5. For the lemon sauce, put the honey, lemon juice, and butter into a small pan and bring to a boil. Boil for a few minutes to reduce, stirring, until syrupy.

6. Serve the cake in slices with the lemon sauce poured over them.

**Serves 6–8**

* oil or melted butter, for greasing
* 1½ cups all-purpose flour
* 1 tbsp baking powder
* ¾ cup strained plain yogurt
  scant ½ cup Greek honey
  ⅓ cup light brown sugar
* 3 eggs, beaten
* 1 tsp vanilla extract

**Lemon sauce**
2 tbsp Greek honey
2 tbsp lemon juice
2 tbsp unsalted butter